THE BEST
OF LEITH'S

THE BEST OF LEITH'S

More than 100 Favourite Recipes from
Leith's School of Food and Wine

Selected by Caroline Waldegrave

BLOOMSBURY

First published in Great Britain in 1998
Bloomsbury Publishing Plc, 38 Soho Square, London W1V 5DF

Text copyright © 1998 Leith's School of Food and Wine

The moral right of the authors has been asserted

A CIP catalogue record for this book is available from the British Library

ISBN 0 7475 4113 2

10 9 8 7 6 5 4 3 2 1

Photographs by Graham Kirk and Andrea Heselton

Typeset by Hewer Text Limited, Edinburgh
Printed in Great Britain by The Bath Press, Bath

CONTENTS

ACKNOWLEDGEMENTS

This book is a compilation of ideas from all the Leith's cookery books; it includes more than 100 of our most popular recipes.

Past and present staff have all contributed enormously to our books and I would particularly like to acknowledge and thank the following people and their books:

Leith's Cookery Bible: Prue Leith, Caroline Yates, Sally Procter, Yan Kit So, Fiona Burrell, C.J. Jackson, Puff Fairclough, Emma Crowhurst, Maxine Clark, Sue Spaull, Eithne Swan and Richard Harvey

Leith's Seasonal Bible: C.J. Jackson and Belinda Kassapian with Philippa Carr for her wine suggestions

Leith's Cooking for One or Two: Polly Tyrer with Richard Harvey for his wine advice

Leith's Easy Dinner Parties: Puff Fairclough and Janey Orr

Leith's Healthy Eating: Puff Fairclough and Ann Heughan

Leith's Complete Christmas: Prue Leith and Fiona Burrell with Richard Harvey for his wine advice

Leith's Fish Bible: C.J. Jackson with Kate McCaulay for her wine advice

Leith's Latin American Cooking: Valeria Sisti with Philippa Carr for her wine advice

Leith's Indian and Sri Lankan Cook Book: Priya Wickramansinge

Leith's Book of Cakes: Fiona Burrell

I would also like to thank all those people who have helped with the production of this book, including Helen Dore who has painstakingly edited many of the Leith's publications, and Monica Macdonald from Bloomsbury who put it together so quickly. The food photographs were cooked by a large number of Leith's teachers, I would particularly like to thank: Puff Fairclough who masterminds the Leith's image, Polly Tyrer, Belinda Kassapian, C.J. Jackson, Barbara Stevenson, Janey Orr, Terry Farris, Priya Wickramansinge and Valeria Sisti. The photographs were taken by Andrea Heselton and Graham Kirk. Finally I would like to thank Annie Simmonds and Claire Smith for very rapid and cheerful last-minute typing.

FOREWORD BY CAROLINE WALDEGRAVE

This selection of more than 100 recipes is taken from the Leith's range of cookery books. They are our favourite recipes and we think that they look as good as they taste. It is quite an unusual collection in that the range is wide: from the common or garden pizza to the supremely elegant Warm Pheasant Mousse with Port Essence. Some of the recipes are old Leith's favourites, such as the Mustard Grilled Chicken; some are new to us, such as Duck Breasts with Spiced Apricots and Red Wine Sauce. Some are very rich, such as the classic Chocolate Profiteroles, but we have also included light, healthy recipes, for example Baked Exotic Fruits.

Whatever you are cooking, be it the humble Lentil Soup or the sophisticated Sablé aux Fraises, it is essential that the basic ingredients are perfect; however technically capable a cook is, bruised strawberries will always be bruised. We would also urge a return to cooking seasonally. It is now possible to get a huge variety of ingredients all year round but we have included some recipes that can only be cooked at the right time of year, such as Fresh Pea Tartlets and Rhubarb Strudel. In fact, we believe most ingredients eaten at the right time of the year taste as they really should.

I do hope that you enjoy cooking from this book as much as I have enjoyed selecting the recipes and photographs. These are the recipes which we believe define our approach to cooking.

MENU PLANNING

Once a menu is planned, cooking becomes much easier. It is making the decisions that can be so daunting. Here are a few hints that may help. One of the most important things is to make the menu relevant to the people for whom you are cooking; giving a rugger XV salad of roast tomatoes would be as absurd as giving a ladies' lunch party partridge with lentils. The menu should stay in style throughout. The figurative leap from the South of France, with terrine de ratatoville niçoise, to the Nursery, with upside-down toffee gingerbread, would also give your guests an uncomfortable culture shock. One of the many skills of cooking is to think of the people for whom you are cooking and choose a menu that you know they will like. Here are a set of guidelines that can help:

- Never repeat the same basic ingredients in a menu – for example, do not have pastry in two courses or serve smoked salmon in the first and main courses. However, it is perfectly acceptable to have a fish first course, such as a seafood salad, followed by a fish main course.
- Try to devise a menu that is full of colour. This is particularly important when planning a buffet party. For a conventional lunch or dinner party, always think about the appearance of the main course plate.
- Think about the balance of the menu. Do not be so inclined to generosity that you daunt your guests. If there is to be a great number of courses then serve a sorbet halfway through to refresh the palate. If you decide to serve a very rich pudding, always offer a light alternative.
- The texture of a meal is important – it should vary.
- Try not to have too many exciting and exotic tastes in one menu. If you get carried away, sometimes the basic flavour of a delicious ingredient can be drowned. If the menu is to include a highly seasoned dish, don't follow it with a subtle dish – your guests simply won't be able to appreciate it.
- Most people love sauces, so if you serve a sauce be generous.
- We would always recommend serving a salad with any rich meal.

At Leith's there is always much discussion about the order of a meal. In England we conventionally serve the pudding followed by the cheese. In France it is more usual to serve the cheese before the pudding – the theory being that the red wine is finished with the cheese and then the pudding is served with a sweet white wine. We rather like the French approach for both its wine appreciation factor and also for its practicality in that it means that the host or hostess can nip off to the kitchen and do any last-minute cooking necessary for the pudding.

Finally, we would say don't overtax yourself. A dinner party is meant to be fun. Don't try to cook three hot courses and sit down to each successive course feeling slightly more flushed. Prepare as much as you can in advance – work out a timetable of how you are going to cope, and enjoy the meal with your guests.

DICTIONARY OF COOKING TERMS

Bake blind To bake a flan case while empty. In order to prevent the sides falling in or the base bubbling up, the pastry is usually lined with paper and filled with 'blind beans'. See below.

Bain-marie A roasting tin half filled with hot water in which terrines, custards, etc. stand while cooking. The food is protected from direct fierce heat and cooks in a gentle, steamy atmosphere. Also a large container that will hold a number of pans standing in hot water, used to keep soups, sauces, etc. hot without further cooking.

Bard To tie bacon or pork fat over a joint of meat, game bird or poultry, to be roasted. This helps to prevent the flesh from drying out.

Baste To spoon over liquid (sometimes stock, sometimes fat) during cooking to prevent drying out and to promote flavour.

Bavarois Creamy dish made with eggs and cream and set with gelatine.

Beignets Fritters.

Beurre manié Butter and flour in equal quantities worked together to a soft paste, and used as a liaison or thickening for liquids. Small pieces are whisked into boiling liquid. As the butter melts it disperses the flour evenly through the liquid, thereby thickening it without causing lumps.

Beurre noisette Browned butter; *see* Noisette.

Bisque Shellfish soup, smooth and thickened.

Blanch Originally, to whiten by boiling, e.g. to boil sweetbreads or brains briefly to remove traces of blood, or to boil almonds to make the brown skin easy to remove, leaving the nuts white. Now commonly used to mean parboiling, as in blanching vegetables when they are parboiled prior to freezing, or precooked so that they have only to be reheated before serving.

Blind beans Dried beans, peas, rice and pasta used to fill pastry cases temporarily during baking.

Bouchées Small puff pastry cases like miniature vol-au-vents.

Bouillon Broth or uncleared stock.

Bouquet garni Parsley stalks, small bay leaf, fresh thyme, celery stalk, sometimes with a blade of mace, tied together with string and used to flavour stews, etc. Removed before serving.

Braise To bake or stew slowly on a bed of vegetables in a covered pan.

Brunoise Vegetables cut into very small dice.

Canapé A small bread or biscuit base, sometimes fried, spread or covered with savoury paste, egg, etc., used for cocktail titbits or as an accompaniment to meat dishes. Sometimes used to denote the base only, as in champignons sur canapé.

Caramel Sugar cooked to a toffee.

Châteaubriand Roast fillet steak from the thick end for 2 people or more.

Chine To remove the backbone from a rack of ribs. Carving is almost impossible if the butcher has not 'chined' the meat.

Clarified butter Butter that has been separated from milk particles and other impurities which cause it to look cloudy when melted, and to burn easily when heated.

Collops Small slices of meat, taken from a tender cut such as neck of lamb.

Concasser To chop roughly.

Consommé Clear soup.

Coulis Essentially a thick sauce, such as coulis de tomates, thick tomato sauce; raspberry coulis, raspberry sauce.

Court bouillon Liquid used for cooking fish.

Cream To beat ingredients together, such as butter and sugar when making a sponge cake.

Crêpes Thin French pancakes.

Croquettes Pâté (stiff purée) of mashed potato and possibly poultry, fish or meat, formed into small balls or patties, coated in egg and breadcrumbs and deep-fried.

Croustade Bread case dipped in butter and baked until crisp. Used to contain hot savoury mixtures for a canapé, savoury or as a garnish.

Croûte Literally crust. Sometimes a pastry case, as in fillet of beef en croûte, sometimes toasted or fried bread, as in Scotch woodcock or scrambled eggs on toast.

Croûtons Small evenly sized cubes of fried bread used as a soup garnish and occasionally in other dishes.

Dariole Small castle-shaped mould used for moulding rice salads and sometimes for cooking cake mixtures.

Déglacer To loosen and liquefy fat, sediment and browned juices stuck at the bottom of a frying pan or saucepan by adding liquid (usually stock, water or wine) and stirring while boiling.

Deglaze See Déglacer.

Dégorger To extract the juices from meat, fish or vegetables, generally by salting then soaking or washing. Usually done to remove indigestible or strong-tasting juices.

Dépouiller To skim off the scum from a sauce or stock: a splash of cold stock is added to the boiling liquid. This helps to bring scum and fat to the surface, which can then be skimmed more easily.

Dropping consistency The consistency where a mixture will drop reluctantly from a spoon, neither pouring off nor obstinately adhering.

Duxelles Finely chopped raw mushrooms, sometimes with chopped shallots or chopped ham, often used as a stuffing.

Egg wash Beaten raw egg, sometimes with salt, used for glazing pastry to give it a shine when baked.

Emulsion A stable suspension of fat and other liquid, e.g. mayonnaise, hollandaise.

Entrecôte Sirloin steak.

Entrée Traditionally a dish served before the main

course, but usually served as a main course today.

Farce Stuffing.

Fecule Farinaceous thickening, usually arrowroot or cornflour.

Flamber To set alcohol alight. Usually to burn off the alcohol, but frequently simply for dramatic effect. (Past tense flambé or flambée; English: to flame).

Flame See Flamber.

Fleurons Crescents of puff pastry, generally used to garnish fish or poultry.

Fold To mix with a gentle lifting motion, rather than to stir vigorously. The aim is to avoid beating out air while mixing.

Frappé Iced, or set in a bed of crushed ice.

Fricassé White stew made with cooked or raw poultry, meat or rabbit and a velouté sauce, sometimes thickened with cream and egg yolks.

Fumet Strong-flavoured liquor used for flavouring sauces. Usually the liquid in which fish has been poached, or the liquid that has run from fish during baking. Sometimes used of meat or truffle-flavoured liquors.

Glace de viande Reduced brown stock, very strong in flavour, used for adding body and colour to sauces.

Glaze To cover with a thin layer of shiny jellied meat juices (for roast turkey), melted jam (for fruit flans) or syrup (for rum baba).

Gratiner To brown under a grill after the surface of the dish has been sprinkled with breadcrumbs and butter and, sometimes, cheese. Dishes finished like this are sometimes called gratinée or au gratin.

Hors d'oeuvre Usually simply means the first course. Sometimes used to denote a variety or selection of many savoury titbits served with drinks, or a mixed first course (hors d'oeuvres variés).

Infuse To steep or heat gently to extract flavour, as when infusing milk with onion slices.

Julienne Vegetables or citrus rind cut in thin matchstick shapes or very fine shreds.

Jus or jus de viande God's gravy, i.e. juices that occur naturally in cooking, not a made-up sauce. Also juice.

Jus lié Thickened gravy.

Knock down or knock back To punch or knead out the air in risen dough so that it resumes its pre-risen bulk.

Knock up To separate slightly the layers of raw puff pastry with the blade of a knife to facilitate rising during cooking.

Lard To thread strips of bacon fat (or sometimes anchovy) through meat to give it flavour, and, in the case of fat, to make up any deficiency in very lean meat.

Lardons Small strips or cubes of pork fat or bacon generally used as a garnish.

Liaison Ingredients for binding together and thickening sauce, soup or other liquid, e.g. roux, beurre manié, egg yolk and cream, blood.

Macédoine Small diced mixed vegetables, usually containing some root vegetables. Sometimes used of fruit meaning a fruit salad.

Macerate To soak food in a syrup or liquid to allow flavours to mix.

Mandolin Frame of metal or wood with adjustable blades set in it for thinly slicing cucumbers, potatoes, etc.

Marinade The liquid described below. Usually contains oil, onion, bay leaf and vinegar or wine.

Marinate To soak meat, fish or vegetables before cooking in acidulated liquid containing flavourings and herbs. This gives flavour and tenderizes the meat.

Marmite French word for a covered earthenware soup container in which the soup is both cooked and served.

Medallions Small rounds of meat, evenly cut. Also small round biscuits. Occasionally used of vegetables if cut in flat round discs.

Mirepoix The bed of braising vegetables described under Braise.

Moule-à-manqué French cake tin with sloping sides. The resulting cake has a wider base than top, and is about 2.5cm/1in high.

Napper To coat, mask or cover, e.g. éclairs nappés with hot chocolate sauce.

Needleshreds Fine, evenly cut shreds of citrus zest (French julienne) generally used as a garnish.

Noisette Literally 'nut'. Usually means nut-brown, as in beurre noisette, i.e. butter browned over heat to a nut colour. Also hazelnut. Also boneless rack of lamb rolled and tied, cut into neat rounds.

Nouvelle cuisine Style of cooking that promotes light and delicate dishes often using unusual combinations of very fresh ingredients, attractively arranged.

Oyster Small piece of meat found on either side of the backbone of a chicken. Said to be the best-flavoured flesh. Also a bivalve mollusc!

Panade or panada Very thick mixture used as a base for soufflés or fish cakes, etc., usually made from milk, butter and flour.

Paner To egg and crumb ingredients before frying.

Papillote A wrapping of paper in which fish or meat is cooked to contain the aroma and flavour. The dish is brought to the table still wrapped up. Foil is sometimes used, but as it does not puff up dramatically, it is less satisfactory.

Parboil To half-boil or partially soften by boiling.

Parisienne Potato (sometimes with other ingredients) scooped into small balls with a melon baller and usually fried.

Pass To strain or push through a sieve.

Pâte The basic mixture or paste, often used of uncooked pastry, dough, uncooked meringue, etc.

Pâté A savoury paste of liver, pork, game, etc.

Pâtisserie Sweet cakes and pastries. Also a cake shop.

Paupiette Beef (or pork or veal) olive, i.e. a thin layer of meat, spread with a soft farce, rolled up, tied with string and cooked slowly.

Piquer To insert in meats or poultry a large julienne of fat, bacon, ham, truffle, etc.

Poussin Baby chicken.

Praline Almonds cooked in sugar until the mixture caramelizes, cooled and crushed to a powder. Used for flavouring desserts and ice cream.

Prove To put dough or yeasted mixture to rise before baking.

Purée Liquidized, sieved or finely mashed fruit or vegetables.

Quenelles A fine minced fish or meat mixture formed into small portions and poached. Served in a sauce, or as a garnish to other dishes.

Ragoût A stew.

Réchauffée A reheated dish made with previously cooked food.

Reduce To reduce the amount of liquid by rapid boiling, causing evaporation and a consequent strengthening of flavour in the remaining liquid.

Refresh To hold boiled green vegetables under cold running water, or to immerse them immediately in cold water to prevent them cooking further in their own steam, and set the colour.

Relax or rest Of pastry: to set aside in a cool place to allow the gluten (which will have expanded during rolling) to contract. This lessens the danger of shrinking in the oven. Of batters: to set aside to allow the starch cells to swell, giving a lighter result when cooked.

Render To melt solid fat (e.g. beef, pork) slowly in the oven.

Repere Flour mixed with water or white of egg used to seal pans when cooking a dish slowly, such as lamb ragoût.

Revenir To fry meat or vegetables quickly in hot fat in order to warm them through.

Roux A basic liaison or thickening for a sauce or soup. Melted butter to which flour has been added.

Rouille Garlic and oil emulsion used as flavouring.

Salamander A hot oven or grill used for browning or glazing the tops of cooked dishes, or a hot iron or poker for branding the top with lines or a criss-cross pattern.

Salmis A game stew sometimes made with cooked game, or partially roasted game.

Sauter Method of frying in a deep-frying pan or sautoir. The food is continually tossed or shaken so that it browns quickly and evenly.

Sautoir Deep-frying pan with a lid used for recipes that require fast frying and then slower cooking (with the lid on).

Scald Of milk: to heat until on the point of boiling, when some movement can be seen at the edges of the pan but there is no overall bubbling. Of muslin, cloths, etc.: to immerse in clean boiling water, generally to sterilize.

Sear or seize To brown meat rapidly usually in fat, for flavour and colour.

Season Of food: to flavour, generally with salt and pepper. Of iron frying pans, griddles, etc.: to prepare new equipment for use by placing over high heat, generally coated with oil and sprinkled with salt. This prevents subsequent rusting and sticking.

Slake To mix flour, arrowroot, cornflour or custard powder to a thin paste with a small quantity of cold water.

Soft ball The term used to describe sugar syrup reduced by boiling to sufficient thickness to form soft balls when dropped into cold water and rubbed between finger and thumb.

Supreme Choice piece of poultry (usually from the breast).

Sweat To cook gently, usually in butter or oil, but sometimes in the food's own juices, without frying or browning.

Tammy A fine muslin cloth through which sauces are sometimes forced. After this treatment they look beautifully smooth and shiny. Tammy cloths have generally been replaced by blenders or liquidizers, which give much the same effect.

Tammy strainer A fine mesh strainer, conical in shape, used to produce the effect described under Tammy.

Terrine Pâté or minced mixture baked or steamed in a loaf tin or earthenware container.

To the thread Of sugar boiling. Term used to denote degree of thickness achieved when reducing syrup, i.e. the syrup will form threads if tested between a wet finger and thumb. Short thread: about 1cm/$\frac{1}{2}$in; long thread: 5cm/2in or more.

Timbale A dish that has been cooked in a castle-shaped mould, or a dish served piled high.

Tomalley Greenish lobster liver. Creamy and delicious.

Tournedos Fillet steak. Usually refers to a one-portion piece of grilled fillet.

To turn vegetables To shape carrots or turnips to a small barrel shape. To cut mushrooms into a decorative spiral pattern.

To turn olives To remove the olive stone with a spiral cutting movement.

Vol-au-vent A large pastry case made from puff pastry with high raised sides and a deep hollow centre into which chicken, fish, etc. is put.

Well A hollow or dip made in a pile or bowlful of flour, exposing the tabletop or the bottom of the bowl, into which other ingredients are placed prior to mixing.

Zest The skin of an orange or lemon, used to give flavour. It is very thinly pared without any of the bitter white pith.

PASTRY

Fresh Pea Tartlets with Walnut Pastry

Serves 4
1 quantity walnut and oat pastry (see page 218)
plain flour

For the filling
15g/$\frac{1}{2}$oz butter
12 small shallots, peeled
225g/8oz shelled fresh peas
salt
2 egg yolks
150ml/$\frac{1}{4}$ pint single cream
1 tablespoon chopped fresh tarragon
freshly ground black pepper

1. Divide the pastry into 4 pieces. Roll each piece out into a circle and use to line 4 × 8.5cm/ 3$\frac{1}{2}$in flan rings. Chill for 30 minutes.
2. Preheat the oven to 190°C/375°F/gas mark 5.
3. Bake the pastry blind (see page 7). Reduce the oven temperature to 150°C/300°F/gas mark 2.
4. Make the filling: melt the butter in a small heavy-based frying pan. Add the shallots and season with salt and pepper. Cover and cook over a very low heat for 20 minutes, or until a skewer slides easily into the centre of the shallots, shaking the pan gently from time to time to prevent the shallots from burning. If the shallots are starting to caramelize a little too much, add a few drops of water and turn the heat down even lower.
5. Blanch the peas in boiling salted water for 2 minutes. Drain and refresh in cold water. Do not allow the peas to sit in the cold water for too long or they will lose flavour.
6. Put the egg yolks, cream and tarragon into another bowl and stir together. Add the peas and season to taste with salt and pepper.
7. Arrange 3 shallots in the centre of each pastry case. Using a slotted spoon, divide the peas between the tartlets and pile them around the shallots. Pour egg mixture over the peas, filling the tartlets up as much as possible.
8. Place the tartlets on a baking sheet and bake near the bottom of the oven for 20 minutes, or until the filling is just set but not brown.

SAUVIGNON BLANC/CRISP DRY WHITE

Pizza

This recipe has been taken from *A Taste of Venice* by Jeanette Nance Nordio.

Makes 2 × 25cm/10in pizzas
10g/^{1}/$_3$oz fresh yeast
150ml/^{1}/$_4$ pint warm water
200g/7oz plain flour
^{1}/$_2$ teaspoon salt
2–3 tablespoons olive oil
1 quantity salsa pizzaiola (see page 216)
225g/8oz mozzarella cheese, diced or grated
3 tablespoons freshly grated Parmesan cheese

1. Cream the yeast with the sugar and 2 tablespoons of the lukewarm water.
2. Sift the flour with the salt and make a well in the centre. Pour in the yeast mixture, the remaining water and the oil. Mix together to make a soft but not wet dough. Add more water or flour if necessary.
3. Turn out on to a floured surface and knead well for about 5 minutes until the dough is smooth. Place in a clean bowl and cover with greased clingfilm. Leave in a warm place until the dough has doubled in bulk.
4. Preheat the oven to 230°C/450°F/gas mark 8. Divide the dough in two. Roll each piece into a 25cm/10in circle. Place on greased and floured baking trays.
5. Crimp or flute the edges of the dough slightly to help keep in the filling. Spread with the pizzaiola sauce. Sprinkle with the cheese and pour over a little oil. (The pizza can be left for up to 1 hour before baking.)
6. Bake near the bottom of the preheated oven for 5 minutes, then turn down the temperature to 200°C/400°F/gas mark 6 and bake for a further 15 minutes.

LIGHT/MEDIUM RED

Leith's Restaurant's Artichoke and Green Olive Pie

Serves 6–8
10 fresh globe artichokes
30g/1oz butter
10 shallots, finely diced
2 small cloves of garlic, crushed
chopped fresh thyme
chopped fresh sage
4 tablespoons dry white vermouth or white wine
150ml/¼ pint double cream
170g/6oz green olives, pitted and chopped
salt and freshly ground black pepper
225g/8oz flour quantity puff pastry (see page 217)
1 egg, beaten, to glaze

1. Peel the artichokes to the core and put them immediately into acidulated water, to prevent discoloration.
2. Preheat the oven to 190°C/375°F/gas mark 5.
3. Cut the artichokes into 5mm/¼in cubes and cook very slowly in the butter, with the shallots, garlic, thyme and sage, until soft.
4. Add the vermouth or wine. Add the cream and reduce, by boiling, to a coating consistency. Stir the sauce every so often to prevent it from catching on the bottom of the saucepan.
5. Add the olives and season carefully to taste with salt and pepper. Leave to cool.
6. Roll out the pastry and use half to line a 20cm/8in flan ring. Pile in the artichokes and olive mixture and cover the pie with the remaining pastry.
7. Brush with beaten egg and bake in the centre of the preheated oven for 15–20 minutes or until golden brown.

NOTE: If fresh artichokes are not available, canned artichoke bottoms may be used.

DRY WHITE

VEGETARIAN

Warm Mushroom, Garlic Caper Salad

Serves 4
225g/8oz large flat mushrooms
110g/4oz shiitake mushrooms
170g/6oz oyster mushrooms
55g/2oz butter
2 cloves of garlic, crushed
3 tablespoons rice wine vinegar
2 teaspoons capers, rinsed
1 teaspoon chopped fresh marjoram
salt and freshly ground black pepper
a selection of salad leaves such as rocket, radicchio,
    frisée, watercress, washed and dried
2 tablespoons hazelnut oil

1. Wipe all the mushrooms carefully. Leave the small ones whole and slice the larger ones thickly.
2. Melt the butter in a large sauté pan, add the garlic and cook over a low heat for 1–2 minutes. Add the mushrooms, increase the heat and sauté for 2–3 minutes, or until just cooked. Tip into a bowl and keep warm.
3. Add the vinegar and capers to the pan and bring to the boil. Remove from the heat, return the mushrooms to the pan and season to taste with salt and water.
4. Put the salad leaves into a large bowl and toss with the hazelnut oil, season with salt and pepper. Add the mushrooms and toss together. Pile into a serving dish and serve immediately.

SAUVIGNON DE TOURAINE

Herb Omelette Salad

Serves 2–4

For the omelette
5 eggs
3 tablespoons olive oil
1 tablespoon chopped fresh parsley
salt and freshly ground black pepper

For the salad
2 red peppers, quartered and deseeded
2 large tomatoes, peeled and cut into strips
1 cucumber, peeled, deseeded and cut into strips
1 head of lettuce
1 bunch of fresh chives, roughly chopped
12 fresh basil leaves, chopped

For the dressing
1 clove of garlic, crushed
2 anchovy fillets, mashed
1 teaspoon Dijon mustard
2 tablespoons wine vinegar
8 tablespoons olive oil
salt and freshly ground black pepper

To garnish
10 small black olives, pitted

1. Make the omelette: in a bowl, mix together the eggs, 2 tablespoons of the oil, the parsley, salt and pepper.
2. Use the remaining oil to fry the omelette. Lightly grease the base of an omelette pan. When hot, add enough of the omelette mixture to cover the base of the pan. The omelette mixture should be the thickness of a pancake. Cook the omelette for about 1 minute. Slide on to a plate and leave to cool. Continue to cook the remaining omelette mixture in the same way.
3. When cool, cut the omelettes into thin strips.
4. Meanwhile, prepare the salad: place the peppers under a hot grill. When charred, hold under cold running water and scrape off the skin, then cut the flesh into 1cm/½in strips.
5. Prepare the dressing: mix together all the ingredients, and whizz in a blender. Season with salt and pepper.
6. Mix together all the salad ingredients, the omelette strips and the herbs. Add the dressing and toss well.
7. Pile on to a serving dish and scatter over the olives.

LIGHT TO MEDIUM RED

Terrine de Ratatouille Niçoise

Serves 10–12
20 large spinach leaves, blanched and refreshed
salt and freshly ground black pepper
2 red peppers
2 yellow peppers
2 green peppers
2 aubergines
1 bulb of Florence fennel
3 medium courgettes
olive oil

For the mousse
olive oil
1/2 onion, roughly chopped
2 cloves of new season garlic, crushed
3 red peppers, chopped

2 tomatoes, chopped
2 tablespoons tomato purée
12 fresh basil leaves
1 sprig of fresh thyme
1 tablespoon caster sugar
150ml/1/4 pint dry white wine
290ml/1/2 pint water
10 leaves of gelatine, soaked in cold water

For the basil sauce
25 fresh basil leaves
150ml/1/4 pint mayonnaise (see page 216)
150ml/1/4 pint single cream
lemon juice to taste
salt and freshly ground black pepper

1. Line a 900g/2lb terrine first with clingfilm, then with the spinach leaves, overlapping them neatly without any gaps. Season lightly with salt and pepper.
2. Prepare the vegetables as follows. Cook the peppers in olive oil in the oven preheated to 220°C/425°F/gas mark 7 for 20–25 minutes. Cool, then remove the skins and seeds. Cut the aubergines into quarters lengthways. Cook in olive oil in the oven for 20 minutes. Peel the fennel, separate the layers and blanch in boiling water for 5–8 minutes. Refresh in iced water and pat dry. Cut the courgettes into quarters lengthways and shape neatly into pencil thickness. Blanch and refresh, then dry.
3. Prepare the mousse: heat a little oil in a large saucepan, and add the onion, garlic, peppers, tomatoes and tomato purée. Add the herbs and sugar, and cook for 4–5 minutes.
4. Add the wine and cook until reduced by half. Add the water and cook gently on the edge of the stove until the vegetables are well cooked (about 15–20 minutes).
5. When cooked, add the soaked gelatine, remove the pan from the heat and allow to cool.
6. Purée the mixture in a blender, then pass the purée through a fine sieve. Allow to cool completely and check the seasoning.
7. Prepare the terrine: pour 2 tablespoons of the mousse into the bottom of the spinach-lined terrine. Cut the yellow peppers to fit and cover the terrine from end to end. Season with salt and pepper as you go.
8. Pour another 2 tablespoons of the mousse on top, then add the aubergine, skin side down first to make a good colour contrast, then another 2 tablespoons of mousse followed by the courgettes. Repeat the process, alternating layers of mousse and vegetable in the following sequence: red pepper, fennel, green pepper, aubergine, yellow pepper. Finish with a layer of mousse.
9. Fold over the spinach leaves carefully to seal the terrine, then cover with clingfilm. Press the terrine with a weight and leave for 8–24 hours in the refrigerator.
10. Prepare the basil sauce: place all the ingredients in a blender and liquidize. Check the seasoning and consistency.
11. Pour a little sauce on to a plate, cut a slice of terrine and place it on the sauce. Serve chilled.

ROSÉ/DRY WHITE

Salad of Roast Tomatoes and Spring Onions

Serves 4
10 medium ripe plum tomatoes
olive oil
salt and freshly ground black pepper
caster sugar to taste
sprigs of fresh thyme
30g/1oz butter
1/2 bunch of spring onions, trimmed and cleaned,
    sliced on the diagonal

For the dressing
1 teaspoon Dijon mustard
2 teaspoons tarragon vinegar
2 teaspoons white wine vinegar
2 tablespoons olive oil

To garnish
3 tablespoons vegetable oil
1/2 bunch of flat-leaf parsley, chopped

1. Preheat the oven to 200°C/400°F/gas mark 6. Cut the tomatoes in half vertically and scoop out the seeds. Drain the tomatoes thoroughly on absorbent kitchen paper.
2. Brush a baking sheet with oil. Arrange the tomatoes cut side up on the sheet. Season with salt, pepper and sugar. Scatter with sprigs of thyme and drizzle over more oil.
3. Roast in the preheated oven for 10–15 minutes until the tomato flesh just gives when touched.
4. Arrange 5 tomato halves, cut side down, on each individual serving plate.
5. Melt the butter in a frying pan and sauté the spring onions for about 2 minutes. Scatter around the roasted potatoes.
6. Whisk the dressing ingredients together, check the seasoning, and drizzle over the tomatoes. Sprinkle with parsley.

Baked Blue Cheese Mushrooms

This dish can be used as a first course, a quick snack served with crusty bread to mop up the savoury juices, or as an accompaniment to a main course.

8 large flat mushrooms, wiped clean
55g/2oz butter, melted
salt and freshly ground black pepper
lemon juice
170g/6oz blue Brie or Cambozola, diced
extra butter for greasing

1. Set the oven to 190°C/375°F/gas mark 5. Brush the mushrooms with melted butter. Season with a little salt, plenty of ground black pepper and lemon juice. Bake for 10 minutes.
2. Put the diced cheese inside the mushrooms. Return to the oven for 5–10 minutes, until the cheese has melted and the mushrooms are tender.

Asparagus and Dill in Jelly

Serves 4
675g/1½lb fresh fine asparagus
570ml/1 pint well-flavoured aspic (see page 214)
1 tablespoon chopped dill

1. Trim and wash the asparagus.
2. In a pan of boiling salted water, cook the asparagus until tender, about 6 minutes. (For this dish the asparagus should be quite tender.)
3. Drain the asparagus and refresh under cold water until cold. Dry on absorbent paper. Trim to the length of a 1.2 litre/2 pint loaf tin.
4. Melt the aspic very gently, then add the dill. Pour about 5mm/¼ inch into the base of a well-chilled loaf tin. Leave to set.
5. When set, arrange some asparagus spears head to tail in a tight single layer on the jelly. Stir the remaining aspic, pour in enough to come a quarter of the way up the asparagus and leave in the refrigerator to set. Arrange another layer of asparagus on the jelly and repeat the process, finishing with a smooth layer of aspic. The tin should be very tightly packed. Leave to become completely set.
6. To turn out the jelly, dip the outside of the tin briefly in hot water. Invert a wet plate over the jelly mould, then turn tin and plate over together. Give a sharp shake and remove the mould.

NOTE: The aspic must always be stirred before it is poured into the tin to ensure that the dill is evenly distributed.

MEDIUM WHITE

Jams Californian Vegetables

This recipe was inspired by Jams Restaurant, New York, where they serve a similar beautifully colourful selection of attractively prepared vegetables.

Serves 4
12 small new potatoes, washed but not peeled
12 baby carrots, or 3 carrots peeled and sliced on
   the diagonal
$1/4$ red pepper, deseeded and cut into 4 strips
$1/4$ yellow pepper, deseeded and cut into 4 strips
4 baby sweetcorn
4 button turnips
16 French beans, topped and tailed
4 broccoli florets
2 courgettes, each cut into 6 diagonal slices
12 radishes
12 strips of cucumber, deseeded
30g/1oz butter
freshly ground black pepper

1. Cook the potatoes and carrots in boiling salted water until just tender. Drain.
2. Blanch all the remaining vegetables except the cucumber in boiling salted water for 2 minutes. Drain.
3. Melt the butter in a sauté pan, add the cucumber and toss all the vegetables in it until lightly glazed. Pile on to a warmed serving dish or divide between 4 individual serving plates and serve immediately.

Couscous Salad with Grilled Aubergines

Serves 6
225g/8oz precooked couscous (see note)
8 dried apricots, chopped
290ml/$\frac{1}{2}$ pint carrot juice or mixed vegetable
    juice
150ml/5fl oz orange juice
2 tablespoons red wine vinegar
1 medium aubergine
$\frac{1}{2}$ tablespoon chilli oil
2 tablespoons olive oil
salt and freshly ground black pepper
3 strips of orange zest
1 bunch of chives, chopped
2 tablespoons pinenuts, toasted

1. Put the couscous and apricots into a large bowl. Put the carrot or mixed vegetable juice, orange juice and vinegar into a saucepan, bring to the boil and pour over the couscous. Leave to stand for 15 minutes.
2. Meanwhile, preheat the grill to its highest setting. Cut the aubergine into 6×1cm/$\frac{1}{2}$in slices on the diagonal. Mix the chilli and olive oils and brush over both sides of the aubergine slices. Season with salt and pepper and grill on both sides until the aubergine is dark golden-brown and soft.
3. Cut the orange zest into thin julienne strips and blanch in a small pan of boiling water for 30 seconds. Drain and refresh under running cold water.
4. Fluff up the couscous with a fork and mix in the chives and pinenuts. Season to taste with salt and pepper.
5. To serve: put a slice of aubergine on to each of 6 individual serving plates and pile the couscous salad on top. Garnish with the orange julienne (see page 8).

NOTE: Most couscous sold in this country is precooked and only requires soaking.

SAINT-VÉRAN

Baked New Potatoes en Papillote

We love these scented potatoes with their slightly crinkly skin. They must be baked in silicone paper rather than tin foil so that they do not steam. They take a surprisingly long time to cook.

Serves 4
675g/1½lb new potatoes, washed and dried
1 tablespoon sunflower oil
salt and freshly ground black pepper
1 sprig fresh rosemary
4 cloves of garlic, unpeeled

1. Preheat the oven to 200°C/400°F/gas mark 6.
2. Place the potatoes on a large piece of silicone paper. Turn them lightly in the oil and season with salt and pepper.
3. Add the rosemary and garlic and wrap the potatoes up in the silicone paper in such a way that the steam does not escape.
4. Bake for about 1 hour, or until tender.

Baked Golden Vegetables

Serves 4
2 yellow peppers
2 red peppers
4 shallots, peeled
4 garlic cloves, unpeeled
2 tablespoons wholegrain French mustard
225g/8oz cherry tomatoes, yellow if possible
1 tablespoon good-quality olive oil
1 tablespoon chopped fresh oregano
salt and freshly ground black pepper
30g/1oz Parmesan cheese, grated

1. Set the oven to 200°C/400°F/gas mark 6.
2. Place the peppers and shallots in a roasting tin and heat in the oven for 20 minutes.
3. Add the garlic to the roasting tin and bake for a further 20 minutes.
4. Remove from the oven and reduce the heat to 180°C/350°F/gas mark 4.
5. When cool enough to handle, remove the stems from the peppers, then peel and deseed, reserving any juices.
6. Peel the garlic, then mash and mix it with the mustard.
7. Place the peppers, shallots and tomatoes in a greased ovenproof dish and spread with the garlic and mustard mixture. Drizzle with the olive oil, sprinkle with oregano and season with salt and pepper.
8. Place in the oven and bake for 15 minutes. Sprinkle with the Parmesan before serving.

MOUSSES, PÂTÉS, SOUFFLÉS

Warm Pheasant Mousse with Port Essence

Serves 6

225g/8oz boned and skinned pheasant, all fat
  removed
1 egg white
570ml/1 pint strong pheasant or white stock,
  made with chicken bones (see page 215)
8 tablespoons tawny port
290ml/$\frac{1}{2}$ pint double cream, chilled
salt and freshly ground white pepper
30g/1oz butter, melted
oil for brushing

For the sauce

1 shallot, finely chopped
150ml/$\frac{1}{4}$ pint white stock, made with chicken
  bones (see page 215)
100ml/3oz dry white wine
110g/4oz chilled unsalted butter, diced
1 tablespoon double cream

To garnish

6 sprigs of fresh chervil

1. Preheat the oven to 170°C/325°F/gas mark 3.

2. Whizz the pheasant with the egg white in a food processor until smooth. Pass through a fine tammy sieve, then chill for 30 minutes.

3. Reduce the stock by boiling rapidly to 6 tablespoons. Remove 2 tablespoons and set aside to cool.

4. Make the port essence: add the port to the remaining reduced stock and continue to reduce by boiling rapidly until only 3 tablespoons remain. Pour into a small container and chill until set.

5. Put the puréed pheasant into a large bowl and set over ice. Stir in the reserved 2 tablespoons reduced stock. Gradually beat in half the cream, then carefully add the remainder and season with salt and pepper.

6. Brush 6 ramekins with melted butter. Chill and repeat with more butter.

7. Spoon half the pheasant mousse into the bottom of the ramekins. Cut the port essence into equal cubes and place a cube in the centre of each mousse. Spoon over the remaining mousse. Cover each mousse with a disc of oiled greaseproof paper and stand the ramekins in a roasting tin half filled with hot water (a bain-marie). Bake in the lower part of the preheated oven for 15 minutes, or until firm and coming away from the edges.

8. Make the sauce: put the shallot, stock and wine into a saucepan and simmer until reduced to 3 tablespoons.

9. Add the butter, piece by piece, whisking all the time. Add the cream and season with salt and pepper, then strain.

10. Turn each mousse out on to a fish slice, drain on kitchen paper, then transfer to the serving plates and pour around the sauce. Garnish with sprigs of chervil.

NEW ZEALAND OR OREGON PINOT NOIR

Red Pepper Bavarois with Red Pepper Salad

Serves 8
3 red peppers, quartered and deseeded
3 small cloves of garlic, finely chopped
1 onion, thinly sliced
1 tablespoon olive oil
salt and freshly ground black pepper
4 large egg yolks
290ml/$\frac{1}{2}$ pint milk
20g/$\frac{3}{4}$oz powdered gelatine
150ml/$\frac{1}{4}$ pint double cream
150ml/$\frac{1}{4}$ pint low-fat plain yoghurt
1 teaspoon chilli sauce

To serve
red pepper salad (see page 214)

1. Preheat the grill to its highest setting. Grill the peppers, skin side up, until they are blistered and blackened all over. Place under cold running water and remove the skins. Cut the pepper flesh into strips.
2. Cook the peppers, garlic and onion gently in the olive oil until soft but not brown. Allow to cool, then purée in a food processor and push through a sieve. Season with salt and pepper.
3. Beat the egg yolks. Put the milk into a saucepan and heat until scalding. Pour on to the egg yolks, stirring all the time. Return the mixture to the saucepan and heat gently until it coats the back of a wooden spoon. Do not allow to boil. Strain into the red pepper purée.
4. Put 3 tablespoons cold water into a small saucepan, sprinkle over the gelatine and leave for 5 minutes until spongy. Lightly oil a charlotte mould or 20cm/9in cake tin. Place the gelatine over a gentle heat until liquid and clear. Add it to the purée. Allow to cool and thicken.
5. Whip the cream lightly and mix it with the yoghurt and the chilli sauce.
6. Fold the cream mixture into the red pepper custard and pour into the prepared mould. Refrigerate until set.
7. Dip the mould quickly into very hot water and turn out on to a serving plate. Serve with the red pepper salad.

MEDIUM DRY WHITE

Cheese Soufflé

Serves 2
35g/1¹/₄oz butter
dry white breadcrumbs
30g/1oz flour
2.5ml/¹/₂ teaspoon made English mustard
pinch of cayenne pepper
290ml/¹/₂ pint milk
85g/3oz strong Cheddar or Gruyère cheese,
   grated
4 eggs, separated
salt and pepper

1. Set the oven to 200°C/400°F/gas mark 6. Melt a knob of the butter and brush out a 15cm/6 inch soufflé dish with it. Dust lightly with the breadcrumbs.
2. Melt the rest of the butter in a saucepan and stir in the flour, mustard and cayenne pepper. Cook for 45 seconds. Add the milk and cook, stirring vigorously, for 2 minutes. The mixture will get very thick and leave the sides of the pan. Take it off the heat.
3. Stir in the cheese, egg yolks, salt and pepper. Taste; the mixture should be very well seasoned.
4. Whisk the egg whites until stiff, but not dry, and mix a spoonful into the mixture. Then fold in the rest and pour into the soufflé dish, which should be about two-thirds full. Run your finger around the top of the soufflé mixture. This gives a 'top hat' appearance to the cooked soufflé.
5. Bake for 25–30 minutes and serve straight away. (Do not test to see if the soufflé is done for at least 20 minutes. Then open the oven just wide enough to get your hand in and give the soufflé a slight shove. If it wobbles alarmingly, cook for a further 5 minutes.)

SPICY DRY WHITE

FISH AND SHELLFISH

Potato Cakes with Smoked Salmon

Makes 8
450g/1lb floury potatoes, peeled and halved
55g/2oz butter, melted
1 egg yolk
salt and freshly ground black pepper
plain flour
1 tablespoon creamed horseradish
2 tablespoons mayonnaise (see page 216)
2 tablespoons soured cream
grated zest of $1/_2$ lemon
225g/8oz smoked salmon, cut into strips

To garnish
55g/2oz salmon roe
1 small bunch of fresh chives, snipped

1. Preheat the oven to 180°C/350°F/gas mark 4.
2. Cook the potatoes until just tender. Drain and cool.
3. Mash the potatoes, add the butter and egg yolk and stir until well mixed. Season with salt and pepper.
4. Divide the mixture into 8 equal pieces and with floured hands shape into flattish circles about 9cm/4$^1/_2$in in diameter.
5. Place on a lightly oiled baking sheet and bake in the preheated oven for 20 minutes, then turn over and bake for a further 20 minutes.
6. Meanwhile, prepare the filling: mix together the horseradish, mayonnaise, soured cream and lemon zest, and season to taste with salt and pepper.
7. Sandwich the potato cakes together with the filling and the smoked salmon. Garnish each one with salmon roe and chives.

VERY DRY WHITE

Ceviche

Serves 4

450g/1lb fillet of monkfish, halibut or salmon, skinned and cut into thin slices or small strips
1 onion, sliced
juice of 2 lemons or 4 limes
1 tablespoon good-quality olive oil
a pinch of cayenne pepper

1 fresh chilli pepper, deseeded and cut into strips (optional)
1 tablespoon chopped fresh dill or chives
1 avocado, peeled and sliced
1 tomato, peeled and cut into fine strips
$\frac{1}{2}$ yellow pepper, cut into fine strips
salt and freshly ground black pepper

1. Put the fish, onion, lemon juice, oil, cayenne pepper, chilli, if using, and half the dill or chives into a dish and leave in a cool place for 6 hours, giving an occasional stir. (If the fish is really thinly sliced, as little as 30 minutes will do; it is ready as soon as it looks 'cooked' – opaque white rather than glassy.)

2. Remove the onions from the marinade.

3. Season with salt and pepper. Arrange on a serving dish with the avocado, tomato and pepper, and sprinkle liberally with the remaining dill or chives.

CHABLIS

Squid Salad with Cucumber and Cumin

Serves 4
450g/1lb squid
150ml/¼ pint water
150ml/¼ pint dry white wine
1 onion, chopped
1 bay leaf

For the salad
1 cucumber
6 spring onions, thinly sliced

For the dressing
1 teaspoon Dijon mustard
2 tablespoons crème fraîche, or Greek yoghurt
2 tablespoons olive oil
½ teaspoon ground cumin
salt and freshly ground black pepper
grated zest and juice of 1 lime
1 tablespoon chopped fresh mint and chives

1. Clean the squid (see note). Chop the tentacles into 2.5cm/1in lengths and cut the body into rings.
2. Place the water, wine, onion and bay leaf into a saucepan and bring to the boil, then simmer for 10 minutes. Strain and bring back to the boil, then add the squid and remove from the heat. Leave to stand for 5 minutes, or until the squid is tender and opaque, then lift out and allow to cool.
3. Peel the cucumber and cut into quarters lengthways. Using an apple corer, remove the seeds and then slice the cucumber into rings about the same size as the squid rings.
4. Make the dressing by mixing all the ingredients together. Check the seasoning.
5. Toss the squid, cucumber, and spring onion in the dressing.

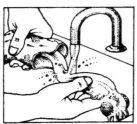 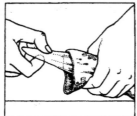

Remove the squid entrails and cartilage

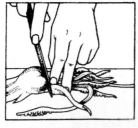 

Cut off the head and scrape away the membrane

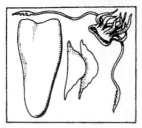

Body, fins and tentacles

Cleaning a squid

Remove the blood (ink) and the entrails under cold running water – they will come out easily. Remove the clear plastic-like piece of cartilage (the quill) that runs the length of the body on the inside. Cut off and throw away the head (it is the round middle bit with two large eyes). Scrape off the pinkish-purple outside skin – a fine membrane – from the body and the tentacles. Don't worry if you cannot get all the tentacles completely clear of it. Wash the body and tentacles to remove all traces of ink: you should now have a perfectly clean, white, empty squid.

DRY WHITE

Skewered Fillets of Rolled Herring

Serves 4
4 × 225g/8oz herrings, filleted (see note on page 78)

For the stuffing
3 tablespoons grapeseed oil
1 clove of garlic, crushed
12 tablespoons fresh white breadcrumbs
55g/2oz Parmesan cheese, freshly grated
1 tablespoon chopped basil
$1/_2$ beaten egg
salt and freshly ground black pepper

For grilling
4 large bamboo skewers, soaked in cold water for 20 minutes
4 tablespoons olive oil

To garnish
lemon wedges

1. Pinbone the herring fillets (see note) but do not skin them.
2. Preheat the grill to its highest setting.
3. Make the stuffing: heat the oil in a frying pan and cook the garlic for 1 minute. Do not allow to brown.
4. Remove the pan from the heat and add the breadcrumbs, Parmesan cheese and basil. Mix well, bind with beaten egg and season to taste with salt and pepper.
5. Lay the herrings, skin side down, on a chopping board. Divide the breadcrumb mixture between the fish. Roll each herring up from the head end towards the tail, like a rollmop.
6. Thread 2 herring fillets on to each prepared skewer. Brush with the oil and season with a little salt and pepper.
7. Arrange the skewers on a baking sheet and grill for 8–10 minutes, turning regularly, or until the herrings are cooked (the skin should be beginning to brown and the flesh should be opaque).
8. To serve: arrange the skewers on a serving dish and garnish with lemon wedges.

ALTERNATIVES: Sardines, mackerel, grey mullet.

TOKAY PINOT GRIS

Lobster Bruschetta

Serves 4
1 French stick, cut diagonally into slices 2.5cm/1in
  thick
2 tablespoons olive oil
1 onion, finely chopped
2 cloves of garlic, crushed
110g/4oz sundried tomatoes, chopped
4 tomatoes, peeled, deseeded and finely chopped
2 teaspoons chopped lemon thyme
salt and freshly ground black pepper
1 teaspoon caster sugar
1 cooked lobster, meat removed from shell and
  diced
12 Kalamata olives

To serve
2 tablespoons freshly grated Parmesan cheese

1. Preheat the oven to 180°C/350°F/gas mark 4.
2. Brush the slices of French stick with some of the oil and bake in the oven until golden-brown. Set aside.
3. Heat a little more oil in a frying pan and cook the onion and garlic until soft. Add the sundried and fresh tomatoes and thyme and season with the salt, pepper and sugar. Cook for 5 further minutes.
4. Add the lobster and heat gently for 2–3 minutes or until hot. Remove from the heat and add the olives.
5. To serve: spoon the lobster mixture on to the toasted bread and sprinkle with a little Parmesan cheese.

WHITE BURGUNDY

Arranged Seafood Salad with Basil Aïoli

This first course is quite extravagant, but ideal for an easy dinner party. For a main course dish, just increase the amount of seafood used.

Serves 8
For the basil aïoli
2 cloves of garlic, crushed
2 egg yolks
a generous handful of basil leaves
salt and freshly ground white pepper
290ml/½ pint grapeseed oil
2 tablespoons lemon juice

a selection of seafood, such as:
16 small oysters, shucked (see note)

16 tiger prawns, cooked, peeled and deveined (see note)
225g/8oz smoked salmon
225g/8oz smoked halibut
225g/8oz smoked mussels
225g/8oz slender asparagus spears
Tabasco sauce
juice of 1 lemon
freshly ground black pepper

To garnish
sprigs of basil

1. Make the basil aïoli: put the garlic, egg yolks and basil into a liquidizer or food processor. Season with a little salt and pepper. Whizz until well puréed. With the motor running, pour the oil in a thin stream on to the egg yolks. When a thick emulsion has formed, add the lemon juice and season to taste with salt and pepper. Pour into a small dish and set aside.
2. Prepare the seafood: remove the top shell of the oysters and cut the smoked salmon and halibut into long strips. Arrange the fish and asparagus in an attractive pattern on a large platter.
3. Season the oysters with a dash of Tabasco. Season the smoked fish with a little lemon juice and pepper.
4. Garnish with sprigs of basil and hand the basil aïoli separately.

Shucking an oyster
Holding the oyster in a cloth, insert a shucking knife at the hinge of the shell. Twist the knife and prise open the shell. Work above a bowl, to catch as much of the juice as possible. Take great care with this tricky operation as if the knife slips it can cause a nasty injury.

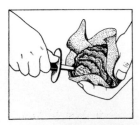

Slip an oyster shucking knife or short kitchen knife under the shell hinge and push and twist it into the oyster.

Deveining a prawn

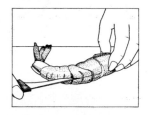 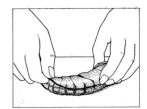

Using a sharp knife, make a small incision the length of the back of the prawn.

Carefully pull away the dark intestinal vein.

After preparing shellfish and other fish, to avoid retaining its odour on your hands, rinse first under running cold water, then wash thoroughly with detergent in hot water.

SANCERRE

Traditional Nori Sushi Rolls

Smoked or raw fish can be included in this simple roll as desired.

Serves 4
2 eggs
1 tablespoon light soy sauce
freshly ground black pepper
1 tablespoon oil
1/2 cucumber, peeled
6 sheets of nori seaweed (see note)
1 quantity sweet vinegar rice (see page 214)

For dipping
3 tablespoons dark soy sauce
1 red chilli, deseeded and chopped
wasabi paste or powder (see note)

1. Beat the eggs and soy sauce together and season with pepper. Heat the oil in a frying pan, add the egg mixture and cook over a low heat until the egg is cooked and resembles an omelette. Remove from the pan and allow to cool.
2. Cut the cucumber into long pencil lengths. Cut the omelette into strips.
3. Lay a sushi mat or thick napkin on a work surface. Using kitchen scissors, trim the nori to fit the mat. Pass the nori sheets through a gas flame to toast them. Lay them on the mat and spoon a layer of rice over two-thirds of each sheet up to the edges.
4. Arrange a couple of cucumber and omelette strips on the rice, then roll up firmly as for a Swiss roll, using the sushi mat or napkin to help you. Press the roll well to compress it and allow it to stand for 15 minutes while you make up the rest.
5. Cut each roll crosswise into 5–6 even slices and arrange on a black or dark unpatterned plate.
6. Mix the soy and chilli together and hand separately in a little dish. Hand the wasabi separately too.

Kombu   A sea kelp that grows in the cooler northern waters of Japan. It is a natural source of the flavour-enhancer glutamate, and in processed form is used in many foods. In Japanese cooking it is mainly used for flavouring and is one of the ingredients in dried fish stock or dashi, along with dried shredded bonito. Like some other seaweeds it is also a natural tenderizer and as such is useful in the cooking of pulses and beans. It also helps prevent beans or vegetables from sticking during cooking.
Sweet kombu   Has a sweet coating and is used for tenderizing soy beans during cooking.
Nori   The best-known of all Japanese seaweeds. Its primary and most popular use is for making sushi. It has a very distinctive sweet, nutty flavour. Nori is very carefully grown in a pollution-free environment. It is hand-harvested, washed, chopped and dried. It can be bought in sheets for use in sushi or in thin shredded strips to coat rice balls, and as a garnish for soups and noodles. It can be mixed with roasted sesame seeds and sprinkled over plain steamed rice.
Wasabi   Japanese green horseradish.

Smoked Halibut with Japanese-style Cucumber Salad

Serves 6
450g/1lb smoked halibut, thinly sliced
finely grated zest and juice of 2 limes
1 small cucumber
2 tablespoons white wine vinegar
2 teaspoons caster sugar
2 teaspoons light soy sauce
1 tablespoon chopped dill
3 tablespoons soured cream
salt and freshly ground white pepper

1. Put the smoked halibut into a shallow dish and add the lime zest and juice. Leave to marinate for 20–30 minutes.
2. Halve the cucumber lengthwise, scoop out the seeds with a teaspoon and cut into very thin strips 7.5cm/3in long. Combine the vinegar, sugar, soy sauce and dill and mix with the cucumber. Leave to stand for 5 minutes.
3. Stir the soured cream into the cucumber and season to taste with salt and pepper.
4. To serve: arrange the marinated smoked halibut on 6 individual plates and spoon a portion of cucumber salad beside each serving.

NEW ZEALAND CHARDONNAY

Lime-marinated Salmon with Papaya

Serves 4
450g/1lb piece fresh salmon fillet, skinned
1 tablespoon chopped fresh dill
salt and freshly ground black pepper
1 papaya
rocket leaves or watercress

For the marinade
1 shallot, finely chopped
zest and juice of 2 limes
1 tablespoon good-quality olive oil
1 fresh green chilli, finely chopped

1. Remove any bones from the salmon and slice on the diagonal into 0.5cm/$1/4$ inch thick slices. Lay the slices in a non-corrosive dish.
2. Mix the marinade ingredients with half the dill, pour over the fish and refrigerate for 2 hours, giving an occasional stir. It is ready as soon as it looks 'cooked' – opaque rather than glassy. (If the fish is really finely sliced, as little as 30 minutes will do; if thickly sliced, it can take more than 2 hours.)
3. When the fish is ready, season with salt and pepper.
4. Peel the papaya, remove the seeds and slice the flesh lengthwise into pieces slightly thicker than the salmon.
5. To serve: Arrange the salmon and papaya on a serving plate in overlapping slices. Spoon the marinade over and sprinkle with the remaining chopped dill. Garnish with rocket or watercress.

CHARDONNAY

SOUPS

Hot and Sour Soup

170g/6oz raw, unpeeled prawns
850ml/1½ pints chicken stock (see asparagus
    jelly)
2 strips lime zest
5cm/2 in piece lemon grass or 2 strips lemon zest
1 red chilli, deseeded and thinly sliced
1 teaspoon light soy sauce
1 teaspoon finely chopped red chilli
pinch soft light brown sugar
1 teaspoon freshly squeezed lime or lemon juice
55g/2oz button mushrooms, very thinly sliced
1 spring onion, thinly sliced
1 teaspoon coarsely chopped coriander

To serve
prawn crackers

1. Peel and devein the prawns (see note), reserving the shells. Put the shells into a pan with the stock, lime zest, lemon grass or lemon zest and sliced chilli. Bring to the boil, cover and simmer for 15 minutes.
2. Strain the stock into a clean pan. Add the soy sauce, chopped chilli, sugar and lime juice. Bring back to the boil, add the prawns, mushrooms and spring onion and simmer for 3 minutes. Stir in the coriander and hand the prawn crackers separately.

Mussel and Saffron Broth

Farmed mussels, now widely available, are much easier and less time-consuming to clean than wild ones.

Serves 6
900g/2lb mussels
570ml/1 pint dry white wine
290ml/$^1/_2$ pint water
1 large onion, finely chopped
3 cloves of garlic, bruised
2 tablespoons chopped parsley
15g/$^1/_2$oz butter
6 shallots, finely chopped
2 large pinches of saffron strands
675g/1$^1/_2$lb ripe beef tomatoes, peeled, deseeded
    and finely chopped
salt and freshly ground black pepper
1 bunch of dill

1. Clean the mussels by scrubbing them well under running cold water. Pull away the beards and discard any mussels that are cracked or that remain open when tapped.
2. Put the wine, water, onion, garlic and parsley into a large saucepan. Bring to the boil, then reduce the heat and simmer for 15 minutes.
3. Add the mussels, cover and cook over a low heat for about 5 minutes until the shells open, shaking the pan occasionally.
4. Drain the mussels through a double thickness of muslin or cheesecloth, reserving the cooking liquid. Discard any mussels that have not opened.
5. When the mussels are cool enough to handle, remove the meat and set aside. Discard the shells.
6. Melt the butter in a large saucepan, add the shallots and sweat until soft but not coloured. Infuse the saffron in 2 tablespoons boiling water and add to the shallots with the strained mussel cooking liquid and the tomatoes. Season to taste with salt and pepper and simmer for 5 minutes. Add the mussels and dill and reheat briefly without boiling.
7. To serve: pour into 6 individual soup bowls.

NOTE: If no muslin or cheesecloth is available use a very clean tea towel.

MUSCADET DE SÈVRE-ET-MAINE SUR LIE

Tomato and Red Pepper Soup

Serves 4
1 tablespoon sunflower oil
1 onion, finely chopped
1 red pepper, deseeded and finely chopped
570ml/1 pint passata
dash Tabasco sauce
2 drops Worcestershire sauce
30g/1oz white rice
290ml/$^1/_2$ pint water
salt and freshly ground black pepper

To serve
2 teaspoons low-fat natural yoghurt
2 teaspoons red pesto sauce (see pages 216–17)

1. Heat the oil in a saucepan and sweat the onion and pepper until soft.
2. Add the passata, Tabasco, Worcestershire sauce, rice, water, salt and pepper and cook for 25 minutes, or until the rice is soft.
3. Place the soup in a food processor or liquidizer and blend until smooth. Return to the pan and leave to simmer for 5 minutes. Taste and season, if necessary.
4. Mix together the yoghurt and pesto sauce and add to the soup, off the heat, just before serving.

AUSTRALIAN CHARDONNAY

Lentil Soup

Serves 4
30g/1oz butter
110g/4oz carrot, diced
55g/2oz celery, diced
1 onion, chopped
110g/4oz potatoes, diced
170g/6oz red lentils, washed
freshly ground black pepper
150ml/¼pint milk
1.1 litres/2 pints ham stock (see page 215) or
    water
freshly ground black pepper

1. Melt the butter in a large saucepan. Add the carrot, celery and onion. Stir over a low heat for about 5 minutes. Add the potatoes and lentils and stir well. Cook gently for 1 minute, then season with pepper.
2. Add the milk and ham stock. Bring to the boil and simmer for approximately 30 minutes, or until all the vegetables and lentils are very soft.
3. Liquidize the soup, then taste and add more pepper or some salt if necessary.

SPICY DRY WHITE

MAIN COURSES

VEGETARIAN

Greek Parsley Pasta

Serves 4
340g/12oz flour quantity egg pasta (see page
   214)
1 bunch of flat-leaf parsley, washed and dried
pesto sauce (see page 216)

1. Roll the pasta out to a very thin rectangle on a lightly floured board. Cut in half. Keep well covered to prevent it from drying out.
2. Take one sheet of pasta and arrange individual parsley leaves at 3cm/1½in intervals, in even rows, all over it. Cover loosely with the other sheet of pasta and press down firmly. Roll again until the parsley can be seen between the layers of pasta.
3. Using a pastry cutter, cut between the rows, making sure that all the edges are sealed.
4. Simmer in boiling salted water for 2–3 minutes or until just tender. Drain well and toss in warm pesto sauce.

MEDIUM RED

Rocket Ravioli with Garlic and Goat's Cheese

Serves 4
225g/8oz flour quantity rocket pasta (see below)

For the filling
225g/8oz hard mature goat's cheese, grated
1 egg
55g/2oz fresh white breadcrumbs
1 clove of garlic, crushed

2 carrots, peeled, grated, blanched, refreshed and
   dried on kitchen paper
salt and freshly ground black pepper

To garnish
3 tablespoons extra virgin olive oil
30g/1oz hard goat's cheese, grated
a few fresh rocket leaves

1. Roll out the pasta as thinly as you can, or if using a pasta machine, pass it through on the finest setting. Using a 10cm/4in biscuit cutter, cut out circles of pasta using enough flour to prevent the pasta from sticking. Cover with clingfilm to prevent drying out while making the filling.
2. Mix all the filling ingredients together and season to taste with a little salt and plenty of pepper.
3. Place a large teaspoon of the filling in the centre of each pasta circle, brush the edges with a little water and fold over to create a half-moon shape. Leave the ravioli to dry out on a large tray sprinkled lightly with flour. Turn them over every 10 minutes to prevent them from sticking to the tray.
4. To serve: bring a large saucepan of salted water to the boil, tip in the ravioli and simmer very gently for about 5 minutes, or until the pasta is *al dente*. Drain, toss with the olive oil and season with plenty of pepper.
5. Transfer to a warmed serving dish and garnish with the grated goat's cheese and rocket. Serve immediately.

ROCKET PASTA

Serves 4

225g/8oz strong 'OO' flour
2 large eggs
2 tablespoons olive oil

1 handful of rocket leaves, washed and dried
salt and freshly ground black pepper

1. Sift the flour into a large bowl, make a well in the centre and drop in the eggs and 1 tablespoon of the oil. Using the fingers of one hand, mix together the eggs and oil and gradually draw in the flour to form a soft dough.
2. Knead until smooth and elastic (about 15 minutes). Wrap in clingfilm and leave to relax in a cool place for 1 hour before using.
3. Cut the dough in half and roll each half out until paper thin, using plenty of flour to prevent sticking. Lay the leaves of rocket out over one half and sandwich them together with the remaining half of pasta.
4. Roll out the 'sandwich' until 1mm/$\frac{1}{16}$in thick. Cut the pasta into 10cm/4in squares and lay out on a wire rack to form a crust (about 15–30 minutes).
5. To serve: bring a large saucepan of salted water to the boil, drop in the pasta squares and simmer for 3–5 minutes, or until the pasta is *al dente*. Drain well and toss with the remaining oil and season with salt and black pepper. Serve immediately.

NOTE: For all pasta recipes use strong 'OO' pasta flour if available.

ITALIAN RED OR WHITE

Ricotta and Vegetable Empanada Pie

Cornmeal is used extensively in many Latin American countries to make cakes, breads, pastries, porridge-type dishes and even drinks. This pastry used here can also be used to make sweet pies filled with apples, pears or quinces.

For the pastry
170g/6oz cornmeal
170g/6oz self-raising flour
1 teaspoon salt
110g/4oz butter
30g/1oz lard
1 egg yolk
4 tablespoons cold water
1 beaten egg, for glazing

For the filling
1 tablespoon sunflower oil

1 onion, thinly sliced
1 garlic clove, crushed
1 red pepper, deseeded and finely sliced
1 green pepper, deseeded and finely sliced
1 red Fresno or Kenyan chilli, deseeded and sliced
$\frac{1}{2}$ teaspoon mild chilli powder
$\frac{1}{2}$ teaspoon ground allspice
1 teaspoon chopped oregano
3 tomatoes, peeled, deseeded and chopped
3 tablespoons chopped parsley
salt and freshly ground black pepper
255g/9oz ricotta cheese

1. Preheat the oven to 200°C/400°F/gas mark 6.
2. Sift the cornmeal, flour and salt together in a large bowl. Rub in the butter and lard until the mixture looks like coarse breadcrumbs. Mix the egg yolk with the water, then add to the mixture. Mix to a firm dough, first with a knife, then with one hand. It may be necessary to add more water, but the pastry should not be too damp. Knead the dough on a lightly floured surface until smooth.
3. Divide the dough into 2 equal parts and line a 24cm/9½in flan tin with one half. Wrap the other half in clingfilm and chill.
4. Meanwhile, make the filling: heat the oil, add the onion and cook over a medium heat for 5 minutes. Add the garlic, peppers, chilli, chilli powder, allspice, oregano, tomatoes and parsley. Mix thoroughly, season to taste and cook over a medium heat, uncovered, for 25 minutes or until the mixture is almost dry. Transfer to a bowl and cool slightly.
5. In a bowl break up the ricotta with a fork and season with salt and pepper.
6. Spread the ricotta mixture into the pastry case. Spoon the pepper and tomato mixture on top. Roll out the remaining pastry and gently lay it on top of the flan. Press the edges together.
7. Cut a few slits in the top of the pie and brush with the beaten egg.
8. Bake in the middle of the oven for about 35 minutes or until slightly browned.

FULL-BODIED RED

Radicchio Risotto

Serves 4

1 red pepper, quartered and deseeded
1 tablespoon good-quality olive oil
2 red onions, chopped
1 clove of garlic, crushed
1 tablespoon freshly chopped rosemary
310g/11oz risotto rice
150ml/¼ pint red vermouth or red wine

860ml/1½ pints chicken stock (see page 215) or vegetable water
450g/1lb radicchio, shredded
8 dried sun-dried tomatoes, soaked in hot water for 20 minutes, drained and shredded
3 anchovies, rinsed very well and sliced (optional)
1 tablespoon pumpkin seeds, toasted (optional)
30g/1oz fresh Parmesan cheese, grated
salt and freshly ground black pepper

1. Heat the grill to its highest setting.
2. Grill the pepper, skin side uppermost, until the skin is black and blistered. Put into a plastic bag, seal and leave to cool.
3. Heat the oil and cook the onion until soft but not coloured. Add the rice and cook, stirring, for 1 minute. Pour in the vermouth or wine, bring to the boil and cook until the wine is absorbed, about 2 minutes. Stir gently all the time.
4. In a second pan heat the chicken stock or vegetable water, and gradually add it to the rice, stirring continuously and gently until all the stock has been absorbed. This can take up to 20 minutes.
5. When the peppers are cool, remove from the bag, peel off the blackened skin and slice the flesh.
6. Add the peppers, radicchio, tomatoes, anchovies (if using) and pumpkin seeds to the pan. Heat through.
7. Remove the pan from the heat and stir in half the cheese. Season to taste and serve straight away with the remaining cheese handed separately.

LIGHT RED

FISH AND SHELLFISH

Dry-Fried Prawns with Coriander

This has been adapted from a recipe by Yan Kit So.

Serves 4
450g/1lb raw, medium shell-on prawns, weighed
    without heads
5 cloves of garlic
2.5cm/1in piece of fresh root ginger
3–4 tablespoons oil
1 tablespoon dry sherry
3 spring onions, chopped
1 tablespoon chopped fresh coriander

For the marinade
$1/2$ teaspoon salt
1 teaspoon sugar
1–2 tablespoons light soy sauce
2 teaspoons Worcestershire sauce
2 teaspoons oil
freshly ground black pepper

1. Using a small sharp knife, slit along the backs of the prawns and remove the black vein. Cut off the legs. Wash and pat dry.
2. Mix together all the marinade ingredients and add the prawns. Leave to stand for at least 30 minutes.
3. Bruise the garlic with a rolling pin, remove the skin and leave the cloves flattened but whole. Peel the ginger and bruise it with a rolling pin.
4. Heat a wok or heavy sauté pan until it is very hot. Add the oil and swirl it about. Fry the garlic and ginger for about 1 minute, remove and discard.
5. Add the prawns. Spread them out in a single layer and fry for about 1 minute. Reduce the heat if they begin to burn. Turn over to fry the other side for about 1 minute. Turn up the heat if necessary. Splash in the sherry. The prawns are cooked when they have turned red and curled up. Sprinkle with the spring onion and coriander. Stir once or twice and serve immediately.

DRY WHITE

Sauté of Plaice with Glazed Kumquats and Garlic

If kumquats are unavailable, lemon may be used in their place. Avoid using very sweet citrus fruits such as oranges.

Serves 4
3 × 450g/1lb plaice, filleted and skinned
1 tablespoon flour
$\frac{1}{2}$ teaspoon salt
$\frac{1}{2}$ teaspoon freshly ground black pepper
30g/1oz unsalted butter
1 tablespoon oil
juice of 1 orange
2 tablespoons brandy

For the kumquats and garlic
8 cloves of garlic, peeled
8 kumquats, thickly sliced
30g/1oz butter
1 tablespoon sugar
3 tablespoons white wine vinegar
1 tablespoon balsamic vinegar
salt and freshly ground black pepper

To serve
1 bunch of watercress

1. Refrigerate the plaice fillets until required.
2. Prepare the kumquats and garlic: blanch the garlic and kumquat slices in boiling water for 3–4 minutes or until the garlic is tender. Drain and dry on absorbent paper.
3. Melt the butter in a frying pan, add the sugar and cook over a low heat until beginning to brown. Add the kumquats and garlic and continue to cook over a low heat until sticky and brown, then add the vinegars. Bring to the boil and season to taste with salt and pepper. Set aside and keep warm.
4. Sift the flour, salt and pepper together on to a plate. Dip the plaice fillets in the seasoned flour. Shake well to remove excess.
5. Heat the butter and oil in a clean frying pan until foaming, then reduce the heat and fry the plaice fillets, boned side down, for 1–2 minutes or until lightly browned and cooked. Take care not to overcrowd the frying pan and avoid burning the butter. As the fillets are cooked, lift on to a serving dish and continue to fry until all the fish is cooked.
6. Deglaze the frying pan: add the orange juice and brandy and scrape up any sediment that may be left at the bottom. Bring to the boil, then season with salt and pepper and quickly pour the liquid over the fish while still sizzling.
7. Spoon the warm kumquats and garlic over the top and garnish with bouquets of watercress. Serve hot.

Filleting a round fish

Round fish are filleted before skinning. If they are to be cooked whole, the skin is left on and peeled away when the fish is about to be served, as in the case of a whole poached salmon. The skin gives flavour to the fish and prevents the flesh from drying out.

To fillet a round fish, lay it on a board. Hold the fish taut against the board with your left hand, and cut through the flesh down to the backbone from the head to the tail. Insert a sharp, pliable knife between the flesh and the bones, and slice the fillet away from the bones, working with short strokes from the backbone and from the head end. Remember to keep the knife as flat as possible, and to keep it against the bones. When the fillet has almost been removed from the fish, you will need to cut through the belly skin to detach it completely.

Some round fish, such as John Dory, with its deep rather than wide body, should be filleted into double or cross-cut fillets. Very large round fish can be filleted into four, following the flat fish method, or the whole side can be lifted as described here, and then split in two once off the fish by cutting down the centre.

Pinboning fish

This is done to remove all the small irritating bones that run along the flanks of the fish, and which are the reason why some people do not enjoy eating fish.

Any cut of fish should be pinboned before cooking. Run the tips of the fingers of one hand over the surface of the flesh to locate the ends of the small bones. Pull the bones out with tweezers or pliers. The fish is now ready for cooking.

PINOT NOIR D'ALSACE

Brill with Deep-fried Vegetable Ribbons

Serves 4
4 × 170g/6oz brill fillets, skinned
30g/1oz butter
1 teaspoon chopped sage
1 clove of garlic, crushed
salt and freshly ground black pepper
1 large courgette
1 large carrot
1 leek
oil for deep-frying

1. Fold each brill fillet into 3, skinned side inside, and arrange, seam side down, on an oiled baking sheet. Set aside.
2. Melt the butter in a small saucepan and add the sage and garlic. Cook over a gentle heat for 1 minute or until the garlic begins to sizzle. Remove from the heat and leave to infuse for a few minutes.
3. Peel the courgette and carrot into ribbons about 2.5cm/1in wide, using a peeler. Put the strips into a colander, sprinkle with salt and leave to stand for 10 minutes.
4. Cut the leek in half lengthwise and remove the outer leaves. Wash well, then cut the leek into long strips 2.5cm/1in wide.
5. Preheat the oven to 180°C/350°F/gas mark 4.
6. Heat the oil in a deep-fryer or large saucepan until a crumb browns within 25 seconds.
7. Rinse the courgette and carrot ribbons, then dry with absorbent paper.
8. Deep-fry a few vegetable ribbons at a time (do not allow to become too brown or they will taste bitter). Lift from the oil and drain on absorbent paper. Sprinkle with a little salt. Keep warm.
9. Brush the brill fillets with the infused butter and grill for 4–5 minutes until the fish is cooked (it should be opaque and firm).
10. To serve: lift the fish from the baking sheet, arrange on a serving dish and spoon over any cooking juices. Arrange the deep-fried vegetable ribbons around the fish and serve.

ALTERNATIVES: Turbot, halibut, sole.

AUSTRALIAN CHARDONNAY

Stuffed Baked Monkfish with Parma Ham

Serves 4

675g/1½lb monkfish tail, filleted
salt and freshly ground black pepper
30g/1oz butter
170g/6oz button mushrooms, sliced
1 teaspoon anchovy essence
1 teaspoon chopped thyme
freshly ground black pepper
6 slices of Parma ham
1 tablespoon olive oil
290ml/½ pint fish stock (see page 215)

For the dressing

4 tablespoons olive oil
4 tablespoons salad oil
2 tablespoons tarragon vinegar
1 tablespoon chopped parsley
1 tablespoon chopped dill
2 teaspoons grainy mustard
salt and freshly ground black pepper

1. Preheat the oven to 200°C/400°F/gas mark 6.

2. Trim the monkfish and remove any membrane. Season the monkfish with salt and pepper and set aside.

3. Melt the butter in a frying pan, add the mushrooms and fry for 5 minutes. Remove from the heat, then stir in the anchovy essence and thyme and season with pepper. Allow to cool.

4. Spread the mushroom mixture on one of the monkfish fillets. Place the second fillet on top.

5. Wrap the monkfish in the slices of Parma ham so that the whole fish is completely covered. Secure the ham in place with string.

6. Brush the wrapped monkfish with oil and put into a roasting tin with the stock. Bake in the oven for 12–15 minutes, or until the fish is cooked (it should be opaque and firm).

7. Meanwhile, make the dressing: combine all the ingredients together in a liquidizer and blend until a green emulsion is formed. Add 2 tablespoons of the cooking liquid. Season to taste with salt and pepper.

8. Remove the string from the monkfish and slice the fish into 2.5cm/1in medallions.

9. Pour a pool of dressing on to each of 4 individual plates. Arrange the monkfish medallions, overlapping, in a semi-circle, on the dressing. Serve hot or cold.

ALTERNATIVES: Swordfish, marlin.

ST-AUBIN BURGUNDY

Citrus-roasted Red Mullet

Serves 4
4 × 225g/8oz whole red mullet, scaled and gutted
2 tablespoons olive oil
grated zest of 1 grapefruit, preferably pink
grated zest of 1 orange
grated zest and juice of 1 lime
2 tablespoons chopped tarragon
salt and freshly ground black pepper

1. Trim all the fins, except the dorsal, off the mullet, and remove the gills (see note). Make 2–3 diagonal slashes into both sides of the fish, nearly through to the bone.
2. Preheat the oven to 180°C/350°F/gas mark 4.
3. Rub the oil and citrus fruit zest into the mullet flesh and arrange the fish in a roasting tin lined with lightly oiled kitchen foil.
4. Pour the lime juice around the mullet, sprinkle with the tarragon and season with salt and pepper.
5. Wrap the mullet loosely in the foil and bake in the oven for 15–20 minutes, or until the fish is cooked (the dorsal fin should pull away easily).
6. To serve: lift the mullet from the foil, arrange on a serving dish and spoon the juices over the top. Serve either hot or cold.

ALTERNATIVES: Grey mullet, sea bream, sea bass, red snapper.

NEW WORLD ROSÉ

Oriental Red Snapper Salad

Serves 4
1.35kg/3lb whole red snapper, filleted and skinned
   (see grilled skewered herring recipe)
2 tablespoons olive oil

For the marinade
1 teaspoon salt
2 teaspoons sugar
1 teaspoon peeled and grated fresh root ginger
1 teaspoon dry English mustard

$^1/_2$ teaspoon ground turmeric
1 teaspoon curry powder (see page 217)
freshly ground black pepper

For the salad
110g/4oz beanshoots
1 red pepper, deseeded and cut into strips
225g/8oz mangetout, blanched
225g/8oz baby sweetcorn, blanched
110g/4oz broccoli spears, blanched

1. Pinbone the red snapper fillets if necessary (see herring recipe). Cut into 5cm/2in chunks.
2. Mix all the marinade ingredients together. Coat the snapper with the marinade and leave, covered, in the refrigerator for at least 2 hours, preferably overnight.
3. Heat the oil in a wok or large frying pan and fry the marinated snapper fillets for 2–3 minutes or until just cooked through.
4. Toss the salad ingredients together with the fish and serve immediately.

NOTE: This can also be served with a hot salad. Just toss the prepared vegetables into the wok after frying the fish and heat through well. Sprinkle with a little sesame seed oil and light soy sauce.

ALTERNATIVES: Red mullet, orange roughy.

NEW WORLD DRY WHITE

Braised Octopus with Glazed Onions and Aïoli

Serves 4
900g/2lb octopus, cleaned (see note)
1 tablespoon oil
30g/1oz butter
1 onion, thinly sliced
1 carrot, thinly sliced
2 cloves of garlic, crushed
2 tablespoons brandy
100ml/3½fl oz red wine

150ml/5fl oz fish stock (see monkfish and parma ham)
salt and freshly ground black pepper
900g/2lb button onions
55g/2oz butter
1 tablespoon sugar

To serve
1 quantity aïoli (see arranged seafood salad recipe)

1. Blanch the octopus in boiling water for 2 minutes, then drain. Peel the dark skin off the main body of the octopus and scrape the skin off the tentacles with a knife. Beat thoroughly with a rolling pin. Cut the tentacles and body into 5cm/2in pieces. Set aside.
2. Preheat the oven to 325°C/170°F/gas mark 3.
3. Heat the oil and butter in a large flameproof casserole. When the butter is foaming, brown the octopus pieces a few at a time. Lift on to a plate.
4. Add the onion and carrot to the casserole, reduce the heat and cook slowly until soft. Add the garlic and cook for 2 further minutes. Put the octopus on top of the vegetables. Add the ink, if any.
5. Heat the brandy in a ladle or small saucepan, ignite and pour, flaming, over the octopus and vegetables. When the flames have died down, pour over the wine and stock and season lightly with salt and pepper. Bring to the boil and cover with a lid. Cook in the oven for 2 hours or until the octopus is completely tender.
6. Meanwhile, blanch the onions in boiling water for 3 minutes, then drain and peel. Take care when removing the skin not to cut too much of the top off, or the onion will disintegrate during cooking.
7. Heat the butter and sugar in a second large flameproof casserole, add the onions, cover and set over a low heat. Shake the pan from time to time, but avoid removing the lid too often. When the onions are well browned all over, put into the oven and cook for 30 minutes or until tender.
8. When the octopus is cooked, lift out of the casserole and stir into the glazed onions. Keep warm. Strain the remaining contents of the octopus casserole into a saucepan, bring to the boil and reduce by boiling rapidly if necessary until syrupy. Season to taste with salt and pepper.
9. Pour the reduced cooking liquid on to the octopus and onions.
10. To serve: divide the octopus, onions and sauce between 4 individual plates. Put a spoonful of aïoli on top of each and serve immediately.

Preparing octopus
Octopus usually comes ready-cleaned. If not, split the top of the octopus in two and remove the ink sac and entrails. Rinse well under cold running water. To skin, blanch the octopus in boiling water for 5 minutes, drain and refresh. Scrape the skin away with a sharp knife. Before cutting up the octopus, tenderize it by beating with a rolling pin or meat mallet.

CHILEAN CHARDONNAY

Salt Cod Ragoût

Serves 4
450g/1lb salt cod
150ml/5fl oz olive oil
2 onions, thinly sliced
5 cloves of garlic, crushed
2 yellow peppers, grilled, deseeded and peeled
2 red peppers, grilled, deseeded and peeled
6 tomatoes, peeled, deseeded and chopped
1 tablespoon chopped thyme
450g/1lb potatoes, peeled and sliced thickly
290ml/$\frac{1}{2}$ pint fish stock (see page 215)

To garnish
12 olives, pitted and halved
1 tablespoon capers, rinsed

1. Soak the salt cod in cold water for 24 hours. Change the water several times to extract as much salt as possible.
2. Drain the salt cod on absorbent paper. Remove the skin and bones and break the flesh into large flakes. Lay on a flat serving dish and pour over the oil. Cover and refrigerate for 2 hours.
3. Preheat the oven to 180°C/350°F/gas mark 4.
4. Heat 2 tablespoons of the cod soaking oil in a saucepan. Add the onions and cook over a very low heat until soft. Add the garlic and cook for 2 further minutes.
5. Cut the peppers into strips and add to the onions and garlic with the tomatoes and thyme.
6. Arrange the potato slices in the bottom of a large casserole and pour over the stock.
7. Lift the salt cod from the oil, mix with the tomato and pepper mixture and spoon on to the potatoes. Cover and cook in the oven for 50 minutes or until the cod and potatoes are tender.
8. Sprinkle over the olives and capers and serve hot.

DRY ROSÉ BORDEAUX

Soy-marinated Tuna on Salad Leaves

4 × 170g/6oz fresh tuna steaks

For the marinade
4 tablespoons sunflower oil
8 teaspoons light soy sauce
large pinch ground ginger
large pinch caster sugar
a good squeeze of lemon juice
freshly ground black pepper

For the salad
assorted leaves, such as watercress, curly endive,
    lettuce, young spinach or rocket
4 teaspoons hazelnut or walnut oil

1. Wash the tuna steaks and pat dry on absorbent paper. With a sharp knife slice the tuna horizontally into three or four wafer-thin slices and arrange in a shallow dish.
2. Mix all the marinade ingredients together and season with ground black pepper. Pour the marinade over the tuna, then cover and marinate for at least 1 hour.
3. Just before serving, wash and dry the salad leaves. Remove any tough stalks. Toss in the nut oil and pile on to a plate.
4. Brush a heavy-based frying pan with oil and heat until smoking. Sear the tuna for 1 minute per side. Set on top of the salad leaves and pour over the pan juices.

White Fish Rostis with Salsa Verde

Serves 4

These are called rostis (rather than fish cakes) because they include grated potato. This, plus the fact that they are low in fat, makes them lighter than conventional fish cakes. Beware that stray wisps of potato do not burn under the grill.

Orange roughy, imported from New Zealand, gets its name from its brilliant-coloured skin. The firm, dense flesh is pure white and tastes delicious, but can be substituted by cod, which may be easier to obtain.

340g/12oz orange roughy, or cod fillets, skinned
2 tablespoons sunflower oil
salt and freshly ground white pepper
2 tablespoons white wine
1 bay leaf
1 onion, chopped
225g/8oz cooked potato
1 tablespoon chopped coriander
1 tablespoon chopped parsley

To serve
salsa verde (see page 216)
lime wedges

1. Set the oven to 200°C/400°F/gas mark 6.
2. Trim the fish fillets and remove any bones.
3. Lightly oil a large sheet of tin foil and place the fish on it. Season with salt and pepper, sprinkle with the white wine and add the bay leaf. Make a loose but tightly sealed parcel with the foil. Place on a baking sheet and bake in the oven for 12–15 minutes, or until cooked.
4. Meanwhile heat 1 tablespoon oil in a saucepan, add the onion and cook until soft but not coloured.
5. Grate the potato coarsely and put into a bowl.
6. Remove the fish from the foil, break into large flakes and add to the potato. Spoon the softened onions into the bowl, then stir in the coriander and parsley. Mix well and season to taste with salt and pepper. Shape the mixture into 4 patties and chill for 15 minutes.
7. Heat the grill to a medium setting.
8. Put the fish rostis on a well oiled baking sheet, brush with the remaining oil and grill for 8 minutes, until golden and heated through. Serve immediately with a spoonful of salsa verde and a wedge of lime.

MEDIUM WHITE/SEMILLON

Roast Cod with Garlic

This recipe is best made with narrow rather than wide fillets of fish.

Serves 4
4 × 170g/6oz cod fillets, unskinned
salt and freshly ground black pepper
seasoned flour
150ml/¼ pint good-quality olive oil
4 cloves of garlic, unpeeled

To serve
lemon wedges

1. Preheat the oven to 200°C/400°F/gas mark 6.
2. Pinbone the cod fillets if necessary (see note). Season with salt and pepper and dip them, skin side down, into the seasoned flour. Shake off excess.
3. Heat the oil in a roasting tin. Add the garlic and bake in the oven for 15 minutes. Remove the tin from the oven and increase the oven temperature to its highest setting.
4. Set the oil in the tin over direct heat and add the cod, skin side down. Let it sizzle for 2 minutes.
5. Turn the cod skin side uppermost, and roast in the oven for 3 minutes or until cooked (it should be opaque and firm).
6. To serve: place the cod, skin side uppermost, on a serving dish with the baked garlic and lemon wedges.

NOTE: If the oil is hot when the fish is cooked in it, the fish will not absorb it.

PINOT NOIR

POULTRY AND GAME

Pot-roasted Poussins with Parmesan

Serves 4
2 double poussins
salt and freshly ground black pepper
2 tablespoons olive oil
30g/1oz butter, clarified (see page 7)
1 large onion, finely chopped
2 cloves of garlic, crushed
2 sprigs of fresh tarragon, bruised
5 tablespoons fino sherry
150ml/$\frac{1}{4}$ pint well-flavoured white stock, made
   with chicken bones (see page 215)

For the sauce
15g/$\frac{1}{2}$oz butter
15g/$\frac{1}{2}$oz plain flour
150ml/$\frac{1}{4}$ pint milk
55g/2oz Parmesan cheese, freshly grated

To garnish
sprigs of fresh tarragon

1. Preheat the oven to 180°C/350°F/gas mark 4.
2. Wipe the poussins and season with salt and pepper.
3. Heat the oil and butter together in a large flameproof casserole. Brown the poussins slowly all over, turning them so that they are evenly coloured.
4. Lift the poussins out of the casserole and set aside. Add the onion to the casserole and cook over a low heat until soft and transparent. Add the garlic, tarragon, sherry and stock. Return the poussins to the casserole, cover with a tight-fitting lid and cook in the preheated oven for 30–40 minutes, or until the poussins are cooked (the juices should run clear when the thigh is pierced).
5. Meanwhile, make the sauce: melt the butter in a small saucepan, stir in the flour and cook for 30 seconds, then remove the pan from the heat and blend in the milk until smooth. Set aside until the poussins are cooked.
6. Lift the poussins from the casserole and keep warm. Strain the contents of the casserole into a bowl and skim off excess fat.
7. Add the fat-free liquid to the sauce and cook over a low heat, stirring continuously until the mixture comes to the boil, then lower the heat and simmer for 2–3 minutes. Remove from the heat and stir in the Parmesan cheese; the sauce should be of a syrupy consistency. Season to taste with salt and pepper.
8. Trim the poussins and cut in half. Arrange on a serving dish and coat with the sauce. Garnish with sprigs of tarragon.

PINOT NOIR

Mustard Grilled Chicken

Although this is called grilled chicken it is partially baked to ensure that the chicken is cooked without becoming burnt.

Serves 4
30g/1oz butter, softened
2 tablespoons Dijon mustard
1 teaspoon sugar
1 teaspoon paprika pepper
1 × 1.35kg/3lb chicken
juice of 1 lemon
salt and freshly ground black pepper

To garnish
a few sprigs of watercress

1. Mix together the butter, mustard, sugar and paprika.
2. Preheat the oven to 200°C/400°F/gas mark 6.
3. Joint the chicken into 8 pieces. Cut off the wing tips and the knuckles. Remove any small feathers.
4. Spread the underside of each chicken piece with half the mustard mixture. Sprinkle with half the lemon juice. Season with salt and pepper. Bake in the preheated oven for 10 minutes.
5. Turn the chicken over and spread again with the mustard mixture. Sprinkle with the remaining paprika, lemon juice and sugar. Season with pepper. Bake for a further 10 minutes.
6. Preheat the grill.
7. Arrange the joints under the grill in such a way that the larger joints are closest to the strongest heat and the breast joints are near the edge of the grill.
8. Grill until dark and crisp but be very careful not to let the joints burn.
9. Arrange the joints neatly on a warmed flat serving dish. Pour over the juices from the pan and garnish with sprigs of watercress.

LIGHT RED

Warm Chicken Salad

This salad can be adapted according to what salad ingredient you have in the refrigerator. It can easily be made into a complete meal with the addition of hot new potatoes. The essential ingredients (other than the chicken) are the rocket, chives, walnut oil and balsamic vinegar. It is also very good made with breast of pheasant instead of chicken.

Serves 4
4 chicken breasts, skinned
seasoned plain flour
salad leaves, such as frisée, lamb's lettuce, gem
   lettuce, rocket
110g/4oz baby sweetcorn
110g/4oz broccoli
salt and freshly ground black pepper
sunflower oil
110g/4oz shiitake or chestnut mushrooms
1 bunch of fresh chives, chopped
4 tablespoons walnut oil
1 tablespoon balsamic vinegar

1. Remove any fat from the chicken breasts, cut the flesh into bite-sized pieces and coat them lightly with seasoned flour. Put them on to a plate, making sure that the pieces are not touching.
2. Put the salad leaves into a large salad bowl.
3. Cook the sweetcorn and broccoli in a small amount of boiling salted water. Drain.
4. Fry the chicken breasts in hot sunflower oil for about 5 minutes, until browned on both sides. Reduce the heat and continue to fry until the chicken is cooked. Meanwhile, fry the mushrooms in a second pan.
5. Lift the chicken pieces on to absorbent kitchen paper.
6. Transfer all the ingredients to the salad bowl, mix together, season well with salt and pepper and serve immediately.

SAUVIGNON

Chicken Breast with Cumin and Mint

Serves 4
55g/2oz sultanas
4 boneless chicken breasts
55g/2oz butter
2 teaspoons ground cumin
2 cloves of garlic, crushed
grated zest of 2 oranges
salt and freshly ground black pepper
30g/1oz flaked almonds
4 tablespoons orange juice

To garnish
freshly chopped mint

To serve
basmati rice or couscous

1. Soak the sultanas in boiling water for 10 minutes.
2. Separate the fillet from the chicken breast and slice the rest into two or three long strips about the same size as the fillet.
3. Melt the butter in a frying pan and brown the chicken on all sides.
4. Add the drained sultanas, cumin, garlic and orange zest. Season with salt and pepper. Toss the chicken over the heat for 5 minutes until tender. Add the almonds and fry for a further minute until brown.
5. Stir in the orange juice, allow to bubble up, then scrape any sediment from the bottom of the pan. Serve immediately with a liberal sprinkling of chopped mint and a helping of basmati rice or couscous.

Sauté of Chicken with Nectarines and Chilli

Serves 4
4 chicken breasts, skinned and boned
seasoned flour
$^1\!/_2$ teaspoon cumin
$^1\!/_4$ teaspoon cayenne pepper
1 tablespoon sunflower oil
1 red chilli, finely chopped
2 nectarines, stoned and quartered (or tinned
    peaches, or dried peaches soaked in water)
5 tablespoons sweet sherry
2 tablespoons water
6 dried sun-dried tomatoes, soaked in hot water
    for 20 minutes, and chopped
1 tablespoon balsamic vinegar
30g/1oz feta cheese, crumbled (optional)
salt and freshly ground black pepper

To garnish
chopped coriander

1. Trim the chicken carefully and cut into bite-sized pieces. Toss in the seasoned flour with the cumin and cayenne pepper, then transfer to a plate in a single layer without touching.
2. Heat the oil in a large frying pan or wok and fry the chicken pieces, in batches if necessary, until golden brown and cooked through. Remove the chicken, then pour off any oil from the pan.
3. Put the chilli and nectarines into the pan with the sherry and 2 tablespoons of water. Bring to the boil and reduce, by boiling rapidly, to a syrupy consistency. Return the chicken to the pan and add the sun-dried tomatoes. Season to taste, add the vinegar and heat thoroughly. Pile into a warm serving dish, sprinkle with the cheese, if using, and chopped coriander.

RED LOIRE

Kukul Mus Mirisata
(Sri Lankan Red Chicken)

In Sri Lanka curries are distinguished by their colour – red, black and white. This red chicken is fiery and hot. The hotness can be reduced by substituting paprika for the chilli powder in the recipe.

Serves 4
8 chicken thighs, skinned, not boned
$1/2$ teaspoon ground black pepper
salt
500ml/18fl oz cold water
3–4 tablespoons oil
2 medium onions, finely chopped
20 curry leaves
8 cloves of garlic, finely chopped
5cm/2in piece of fresh root ginger, peeled and
   grated
3 teaspoons chilli powder
1 teaspoon paprika
2 teaspoons granulated sugar

1. Put the chicken, pepper and salt to taste into a saucepan with the water, and bring to the boil. Cover, lower the heat and simmer for 1 hour.
2. Remove the pieces of chicken to a plate. Bring the cooking stock rapidly to the boil and boil until reduced to about 150ml/$1/4$ pint. Set aside.
3. Heat the oil in a medium saucepan. Add the onion and curry leaves, garlic and ginger, and fry until the onions are golden-brown. Add the chicken pieces and fry for a further 2–3 minutes. Add the chilli powder, paprika, sugar and chicken stock and bring slowly to the boil. Cover and simmer for 5–7 minutes, stirring occasionally to prevent the chicken from sticking to the pan.

Grinding/blending equipment
Spices need to be ground into a fine powder and mixed prior to use; grain needs to be ground into flour; and often a variety of ingredients need to be ground with liquid to form a smooth paste. The traditional chef has several appliances to help in these varied tasks. Most widely used is the stone mortar and pestle, of which there are several types. Another device used for much the same purpose is the grinding stone. This is used for pounding grain or for mixing ingredients to form a paste. A mortar and pestle is a feasible import into the Western kitchen and one that I strongly recommend. However, most of the grinding and blending required in Indian cooking is now most conveniently done using an electric grinder, a blender or a food processor.

Duck Breasts with Spiced Apricot and Red Wine Sauce

Serves 4
2 large duck breasts, boned
salt and freshly ground black pepper
30g/1oz caster sugar
12 firm fresh apricots, halved and stones removed

For the sauce
15g/^{1}/$_2$oz butter
4 shallots, finely chopped
1 clove of garlic, crushed
1 teaspoon ground mixed spice
150ml/^{1}/$_4$ pint red wine
290ml/^{1}/$_2$ pint white stock, made with chicken
   bones (see page 215)
1 tablespoon redcurrant jelly

To garnish
1 bunch of watercress

1. Trim the duck breasts of any membranes or sinew. Score the skin side in a criss-cross pattern with a sharp knife and season well with salt and pepper.
2. Make the sauce: melt the butter in a heavy-based saucepan, add the shallots and fry until golden. Add the garlic and mixed spice and cook for a further minute. Pour in the wine and boil until reduced to 3 tablespoons. Add the stock.
3. Heat a heavy-based frying pan and place the duck breasts in it, skin side down. Fry over a high heat for at least 5–8 minutes, possibly longer depending on the size of the duck breasts, until the skin is well browned. As the duck skin browns it will release a lot of fat which should be tipped out of the frying pan at intervals or the skin will not become crispy.
4. Turn the duck breasts over in the pan, lower the heat and continue to cook for a further 2 minutes. If you do not like duck served pink, continue to cook for a further 5 minutes. Transfer the duck breasts to a plate and keep warm.
5. Tip the fat out of the frying pan and wipe out with kitchen paper. Strain the sauce into the pan and reduce by boiling rapidly, stirring to release any sediment from the bottom of the pan, until the sauce has a syrupy consistency. Meanwhile, skim off any scum that rises to the surface.
6. Pour 2 tablespoons of the duck fat into a separate frying pan. Add the sugar and heat until caramelized. Put the apricots into the pan and fry them, turning them over occasionally, until they caramelize and start to soften.
7. To serve: slice the duck breasts very thinly and arrange, overlapping, on a warmed serving dish with the apricots. Pour the red wine sauce around and garnish with the watercress.

TOP ESTATE NEW ZEALAND PINOT NOIR

Warm Pigeon Breast and Cracked Wheat Salad

Serves 6
12 pigeon breasts, skinned
170g/6oz cracked wheat or bulghar
3 tablespoons sesame oil
$1/2$ red chilli, deseeded and finely chopped
2.5cm/1in piece of fresh root ginger, peeled and
    grated
110g/4oz shiitake mushrooms, sliced
110g/4oz Parma ham, sliced
140g/5oz plum jam
5 spring onions, sliced on the diagonal
55g/2oz sun-dried tomatoes in oil, drained and
    sliced
salt and freshly ground black pepper
lemon juice
30g/1oz pinenuts, toasted
$1/2$ cucumber, deseeded and finely chopped
2 tablespoons oil

For the marinade
2 tablespoons Chinese five-spice powder
1 tablespoon light soy sauce

To garnish
2 tablespoons snipped chives

1. Mix together the marinade ingredients and coat the pigeon breasts on both sides. Put into a shallow dish, cover and leave to marinate for at least 30 minutes or overnight in the refrigerator.
2. Put the cracked wheat or bulghar into a bowl and cover with cold water. Leave to stand for 15 minutes. Drain thoroughly, squeeze out any remaining water and spread out to dry on absorbent paper.
3. Heat the sesame oil in a wok or large frying pan, add the chilli, ginger, mushrooms and Parma ham and stir-fry over a high heat for 2–3 minutes. Add the jam, spring onions and sun-dried tomatoes and bring to the boil. Add the cracked wheat and season to taste with salt, pepper and lemon juice. Heat thoroughly and stir in the pinenuts and cucumber. Keep warm.
4. Heat the oil in a frying pan, add the pigeon breasts in batches and fry for 3 minutes. Turn and cook for 2 further minutes until browned but pink inside.
5. To serve: place 2 pigeon breasts on each of 6 individual plates and spoon a portion of the cracked wheat salad beside each serving. Sprinkle with the chives.

ALSACE GEWÜRZTRAMINER

Quail Braised with Red Cabbage and Plums

8 quail
salt and freshly ground black pepper
16 juniper berries
1 red cabbage
2 red onions
225g/8oz fresh plums
3 tablespoons olive oil
55g/2oz sultanas
4 teaspoons brown sugar
4 teaspoons wine vinegar

1. Wash the quail. Season inside and out with salt and pepper. Crush the juniper berries and put one berry inside each quail.
2. Remove the stalk from the cabbage and slice the leaves finely. Immerse in cold water. Peel and finely slice the red onion. Stone and chop the plums roughly.
3. Heat the olive oil in a large, heavy-based pan and brown the quail all over. Set aside. Fry the onion gently until softened.
4. Drain the cabbage and place in the pan. Add the plums, sultanas, sugar, vinegar and remaining juniper berries. Season with salt and pepper and stir well.
5. Place the quail in the pan, embedding them well into the cabbage. Cover and simmer gently for 40 minutes, shaking and stirring from time to time. The cabbage should be dark and well cooked with all the liquid evaporated and the quail tender.

Pheasant en Papillote

Serves 4
4 × 170g/6oz pheasant breasts, skin removed
freshly ground black pepper
8 rindless rashers streaky bacon
2 tablespoons chopped fresh rosemary
oil for brushing
4 teaspoons redcurrant jelly

To serve
bread sauce (see page 215)

1. Preheat the oven to 200°C/400°F/gas mark 6. Preheat the grill to its highest setting.
2. Season the pheasant breasts well with pepper.
3. Lay 2 rashers of bacon side by side on a board and stretch them out with the back of a knife. Sprinkle over ½ tablespoon of the rosemary. Lay a pheasant breast at one end and roll up, securing the bacon with a wooden cocktail stick. Repeat with the remaining pheasant breasts.
4. Lay the pheasant breasts on a baking sheet and grill for 3 minutes on each side until the bacon is golden-brown. Set aside to cool.
5. Cut out 4 × 30cm/12in greaseproof paper circles. Take a circle and brush with oil. Lay a pheasant breast on one side of the paper. Spread with 1 teaspoon of redcurrant jelly. Fold over the greaseproof paper to enclose the pheasant breast and twist the edges of the paper together so it is completely sealed.
6. Repeat with the remaining pheasant breasts.
7. Place the parcels on a baking sheet and bake at the top of the preheated oven for 10 minutes.
8. Place the parcels on individual plates and leave for the diners to open. Hand the bread sauce separately.

CLARET

Venison Burgers with Sour Cherry Relish

Serves 4
450g/1lb venison fillet
110g/4oz pork fat, minced
salt and freshly ground black pepper
1 tablespoon finely chopped fresh sage
1 tablespoon Worcestershire sauce
1 tablespoon whisky
1 small onion, grated
1 clove of garlic, crushed
2 tablespoons olive oil

For the relish
110g/4oz dried sour Montmorency cherries
5 tablespoons water
1 red chilli, finely chopped
2 tablespoons rice wine vinegar
grated zest and juice of 1 orange
3 tablespoons soft dark brown sugar
salt and freshly ground black pepper

To serve
wholemeal bread rolls
small sprigs of fresh sage

1. Trim the venison of any membrane. Put into a food processor and whizz until finely chopped. Transfer to a bowl and mix with all the remaining ingredients except the oil.
2. Preheat the grill to its highest setting.
3. Meanwhile, make the relish: put all the ingredients into a saucepan and bring to the boil, then lower the heat and simmer for 15–20 minutes, or until the liquid has evaporated and the cherries are sticky. Do not allow to burn.
4. Shape the minced venison into 4 burgers, brush with oil and season with salt and pepper. Grill on the second grill shelf for 2–3 minutes on each side, or until just cooked.
5. Cut the bread rolls in half and toast under the grill. Divide the burgers and relish between the rolls. Garnish with the sage and serve very hot.

CHÂTEAUNEUF DU PAPE

Venison Steaks with Lemon and Redcurrant Sauce

Serves 4
For the sauce
1 lemon
110g/4oz redcurrant jelly
1 cinnamon stick
2 tablespoons port
45g/1½oz butter, chilled and cut into small pieces

For the steaks
4 × 1cm/½in venison steaks cut from the leg or
    loin
salt and freshly ground black pepper
1 tablespoon juniper berries, crushed
55g/2oz butter
2 tablespoons olive oil
4 tablespoons port

To garnish
1 small bunch of watercress

1. First prepare the sauce: pare the zest from the lemon and cut into fine needleshreds. Cut the lemon in half and squeeze the juice. Reserve.
2. Heat the redcurrant jelly gently with the cinnamon stick, port and needleshreds. Simmer for 10 minutes, then add the strained lemon juice and beat in the butter.
3. Trim the venison steaks of any tough membranes and season them with salt, pepper and juniper berries.
4. Heat the butter and oil in a heavy frying pan and cook the steaks over a high heat to brown on both sides. Reduce the heat and cook for a total of about 8 minutes, depending on size.
5. Remove the steaks to a warmed serving dish. Pour the fat out of the frying pan and deglaze with the port. Pour over the steaks.

FULL RED

Partridge with Lentils

2 partridges, drawn, trussed and larded
salt
30g/1oz lard
30g/1oz rindless unsmoked bacon, chopped
30g/1oz onion, chopped
110g/4oz Puy lentils, soaked in cold water for 1
    hour and drained
grated zest of 1/2 lemon
1 bay leaf
110g/4oz Gyula sausage or similar dried, smoked
    pork sausage
290ml/1/2 pint white stock, made with chicken
    bones (see asparagus and dill recipe)
75ml/3fl oz soured cream

1. Preheat the oven to 170°C/325°F/gas mark 3.
2. Sprinkle the partridges with salt. Melt the lard in a large frying pan and fry the partridges until they are golden-brown all over. Remove from the pan.
3. Fry the bacon and onion in the same pan until golden-brown.
4. Put the lentils into a large casserole with the lemon zest and bay leaf. Add the partridges, sausage, bacon and onion. Pour over enough stock to just cover the ingredients. Cover with a lid and cook in the preheated oven until the partridges are tender (about 45 minutes). If the partridges are ready before the lentils, remove them and the sausages from the pan.
5. When the lentils are tender, pour over the soured cream and bring the liquid to the boil.
6. Carve the partridges and cut the sausages into thin slices. Place the lentils in a deep serving dish, put the partridge pieces on top and garnish with the sliced sausage.

RED BURGUNDY

MEAT AND OFFAL

Spiced Beef with Tropical Fruits

Serves 4
900g/2lb chuck or skirt steak
2 tablespoons olive oil
30g/1oz butter
2 large onions, thinly sliced
4 cloves of garlic, crushed
5cm/2in piece of fresh root ginger, peeled and
    finely chopped
2 teaspoons cumin seeds
8 dried chillies
1 teaspoon coriander seeds
1 teaspoon ground turmeric
1 teaspoon garam masala
30g/1oz creamed coconut

30g/1oz sweet tamarind
5 tablespoons boiling water
290ml/$\frac{1}{2}$ pint brown stock (see pages 214–15)
salt and freshly ground black pepper

To serve
1 papaya
1 large plantain or 2 small unripe bananas
3 tablespoons chopped fresh coriander

To garnish
a few sprigs of fresh coriander

1. Preheat the oven to 170°C/325°F/gas mark 3.
2. Trim the meat of excess fat and gristle and cut across the grain into 5cm/2in steaks.
3. Heat the oil in a large flameproof casserole and brown the meat a few pieces at a time. Lift out and set aside and continue in the same way until all the meat is browned.
4. Add the butter to the casserole, lower the heat and add the onions. Cover and cook over a very low heat until the onions are very soft and golden-brown (this may take up to 45 minutes).
5. Meanwhile, put the garlic, ginger, cumin seeds, chillies, coriander seeds and 2 tablespoons of the stock into a blender and whizz to form a paste.
6. When the onions are cooked, add the chilli paste, increase the heat and cook for 5 minutes. Add the turmeric, garam masala and creamed coconut and continue to cook for a further minute.
7. Put the tamarind into a bowl and cover with the boiling water. Stir well and strain the liquid into the contents of the casserole. Discard the remaining pulp.
8. Add the remaining stock to the casserole, season lightly with salt and pepper and bring to the boil. Cover and cook in the preheated oven for 1$\frac{1}{2}$–2 hours, or until the meat is tender.
9. Prepare the fruit: peel the papaya and cut into thick slices and peel and slice the plantain or bananas.
10. When the meat is cooked, lift from the casserole and boil the sauce rapidly until it is of a syrupy consistency. Return the meat to the casserole, add the fruit and heat until the fruit is hot. Season to taste with salt and pepper and stir in the coriander. Arrange in a warmed serving dish and garnish with the sprigs of coriander. Serve very hot.

BEER

Gaeng Ped Nua (Spicy Red Beef)

Ingredients for this recipe are available in specialist Thai shops.

Serves 6–8
2 tablespoons Thai red curry paste
3 tablespoons oil
1.35kg/3lb braising steak, cut into strips
1 stalk of lemon grass, cut into strips
a few makrut (citrus) leaves
340g/12oz creamed coconut
2 tablespoons nam pla (Thai fish bouillon)
$\frac{1}{2}$ teaspoon sugar
2 red peppers, cored, deseeded and cut into strips
1 bunch of fresh basil

1. Fry the curry paste in the oil in a large work or pan for 1 minute. Add the strips of beef and stir-fry, then, ensuring that the curry paste coats the meat, cover with water and add the lemon grass and broken-up makrut leaves.
2. Simmer until the beef is tender (about $1\frac{1}{2}$ hours).
3. Mix the creamed coconut with 570ml/1 pint water and add it to the pan. Reduce until the sauce is thick.
4. Add the fish bouillon, sugar and red peppers and simmer until the peppers are just cooked.
5. Finally add the basil leaves.
6. Serve with steamed or boiled rice.

NOTE: If the sauce curdles (which it often does) it can be brought back with vigorous whisking.

FULL SPICY RED

Fillet Steaks with Parsnip and Sesame Cakes

Serves 6
6 × 170g/6oz fillet steaks
2 tablespoons sesame oil
1 medium onion, finely chopped
4 medium parsnips, peeled and grated
2 tablespoons crème fraîche or double cream
2 tablespoons sesame seeds, toasted
1 tablespoon snipped chives
salt and freshly ground black pepper

1. Trim the fillet steaks of any fat and sinew.
2. Preheat the oven to 200°C/400°F/gas mark 6.
3. Heat 1 tablespoon of the oil in a large frying pan, add the onion and sweat until soft but not coloured. Add the parsnips and cook for 4–5 minutes until opaque.
4. Stir in the crème fraîche or cream, sesame seeds and chives and season to taste with salt and pepper. Divide the mixture between 12 lightly greased patty tins.
5. Bake in the oven for about 15 minutes or until golden-brown.
6. Meanwhile, heat the remaining oil in a large frying pan, add the steaks and cook over a high heat for 5–8 minutes, depending on thickness, until brown on the outside and pink in the centre.
7. To serve: place a steak and 2 parsnip cakes on each of 6 individual plates and serve immediately.

VOSNE-ROMANÉE

Stir-fried Beef Japanese-style with Ginger and Orange Glaze

This recipe calls for Japanese soy sauce; if it is not available, light soy sauce is the best substitute. If you cannot obtain mirin (Japanese rice wine), light muscovado sugar or a sweet sherry can be used instead.

Serves 4
675g/1½lb lean beef (sirloin or rump)
2 tablespoons sunflower oil
140g/5oz French beans, trimmed
110g/4oz carrots, cut into julienne strips
salt and freshly ground black pepper
1 tablespoon sesame seeds, toasted

For the marinade
2 tablespoons Japanese soy sauce
2 tablespoons port
2 tablespoons mirin
grated zest and juice of 1 orange
1 dried chilli
1 tablespoon honey
1 tablespoon orange flower water
2.5cm/1 inch fresh ginger, grated

1. Place all the marinade ingredients in a small saucepan. Bring slowly to the boil, then simmer for 3 minutes, or until syrupy. Remove from the heat and leave to cool.
2. Slice the beef across the grain into thread-like strips 7.5cm/3 inches long. Place in a bowl with the marinade, then cover and refrigerate overnight.
3. Lift the beef from the marinade with a slotted spoon. Strain and reserve the marinade.
4. Heat half the oil in a wok, add the beans and marinade and cook for 2 minutes. Remove and keep warm.
5. Heat the remaining oil in the wok. Add half the beef, increase the heat and stir-fry until cooked but tender, about 2 minutes. Remove, keep warm and cook the remaining beef in the same way.
6. Return all the beef plus the beans and carrots to the wok and cook until hot and the juices are syrupy. Season to taste. Pile on to a warmed serving dish, scatter with sesame seeds and serve.

LIGHT RED

Minted Lamb Casserole with Redcurrants and Port

This recipe needs to be started a day in advance of serving.

Serves 4
900g/2lb lamb neck fillet, trimmed
sunflower oil for frying
1 tablespoon plain flour
290ml/^{1}/$_2$ pint brown stock (see pages 214–15)
salt and freshly ground black pepper
150ml/^{1}/$_4$ pint port

For the marinade
2 onions, thinly sliced
1 clove of garlic, bruised
750ml/1 bottle red wine
1 bay leaf

To garnish
110g/4oz redcurrants
55g/2oz sugar
1 bunch of fresh mint, shredded

1. Cut the lamb into 4cm/1^1/$_2$in pieces and place in a bowl. Add the marinade ingredients, cover and leave overnight, turning the lamb from time to time.
2. Drain the lamb, reserving the marinade.
3. Preheat the oven to 150°C/300°F/gas mark 2.
4. Heat 1 tablespoon oil in a frying pan and brown the lamb, a few pieces at a time. Deglaze the pan with some water between batches if it starts to burn. Add a little more oil to the pan and fry the onions from the marinade until golden-brown. Crush the garlic from the marinade, add to the pan and cook for 1 further minute.
5. Stir the flour into the onions, then add the reserved marinade. Bring to the boil, then lower the heat and simmer for 2 minutes.
6. Tip into a casserole with the stock and any extra water needed to cover the lamb. Season well with salt and pepper, cover with a close-fitting lid and cook at the bottom of the preheated oven for 1^1/$_2$ hours, or until the lamb is tender.
7. Strain the juices into a frying pan, add the port and reduce by boiling rapidly until syrupy. Tip the sauce back into the casserole. Check the seasoning.
8. Put the redcurrants, sugar and 2 tablespoons of water into a small saucepan and heat gently. Sprinkle them on to the casserole with the mint and serve immediately.

RIOJA RESERVA

Rack of Lamb with Lettuce and Beans

2 × 6 cutlet rack of lamb, chined, trimmed and
   skinned
4 teaspoons wholegrain mustard
4 teaspoons brown sugar
salt and freshly ground black pepper
handful washed and shredded crisp lettuce
2 × 225g/8oz tin butter beans
1 tablespoon fresh chopped mint

1. Set the oven to 220°C/425°F/gas mark 7. Trim the excess fat from the lamb. Using a sharp
knife, score the remaining fat with criss-cross slashes. Spread the mustard over the skin, then
press on the brown sugar. Season with salt and pepper. Roast for 10–15 minutes for slightly
pink meat.
2. Dry the lettuce well with absorbent paper. Drain the butter beans. Lift the lamb on to a
warm plate. Pour off the excess fat from the roasting tin and set the pan over the heat on top of
the stove. Add the lettuce and beans. Season with salt and pepper. Toss over the heat in the pan
juices, until the lettuce is wilted and the beans are hot. Stir in the chopped mint and spoon on
to the plate beside the lamb.

Noisettes of Lamb with Apricot and Caper Jam

Serves 6
12 × 85g/3oz lamb noisettes
olive oil
salt and freshly ground black pepper

For the apricot and caper jam
1 tablespoon olive oil
1 Spanish onion, sliced
5 tablespoons dry white wine
225g/8oz no-need-to-soak dried apricots, roughly
   chopped
1 tablespoon mustard seeds
$1/_2$ tablespoon finely chopped rosemary
a pinch of cayenne pepper
1 tablespoon cider vinegar
2 tablespoons capers, rinsed and drained
salt and freshly ground black pepper

1. Make the apricot and caper jam: heat the oil in a large saucepan, add the onion and sweat over a low heat until soft but not coloured. Add the wine and reduce by boiling rapidly to half its original quantity. Add the apricots, mustard seeds, rosemary and cayenne and cook until the apricots are soft and the liquid syrupy. Add the vinegar and capers and season to taste with salt and pepper.
2. Preheat the grill to its highest setting. Drizzle a little oil on the lamb noisettes and season lightly with salt and pepper. Grill for 5 minutes on each side (the meat should be slightly pink in the centre). Serve immediately with a spoonful of warm apricot and caper jam on each plate.

GIGONDAS

Shoulder of Lamb 'en Ballon'

This dish is served with a sweet port gravy.

Serves 6–8
1 boned shoulder of lamb
salt and freshly ground black pepper
sprigs of fresh rosemary
290ml/½ pint brown stock made with lamb bones
    or water
150ml/5fl oz port

For the seasoning in the centre of the lamb
2 tablespoons chopped fresh parsley
85g/3oz smoked ham, chopped
salt and freshly ground black pepper

For the glaze
2 tablespoons redcurrant jelly

To garnish
watercress

1. Preheat the oven to 190°C/375°F/gas mark 5.
2. Mix the seasoning ingredients together and push into the lamb, or, if the lamb has been opened out, spread it on one half and fold the other half over to cover it.
3. Using a long piece of string, tie the shoulder so that the indentations made by the string resemble the grooves in a melon or the lines between the segments of a beachball (see note).
4. Weigh the lamb and calculate the cooking time at 20 minutes per 450g/1lb plus 20 minutes.
5. Sprinkle with salt and pepper. Scatter a few rosemary leaves on top. Pour the stock into the pan.
6. Roast in the preheated oven for its calculated cooking time. Half an hour before the end of cooking, smear the lamb with redcurrant jelly and return to the oven.
7. Remove the string carefully and lift the lamb on to a warmed serving dish. Leave to rest for 15 minutes before serving. It will retain heat even if not placed in a warming cupboard.
8. Meanwhile, make the gravy: skim the fat from the juices in the pan. Add the port and bring to the boil. Boil vigorously until the sauce is syrupy and reduced to about 200ml/7fl oz. Check the seasoning. Strain into a warmed gravy-boat. Garnish the lamb with watercress and serve with the gravy.

Lamb 'en ballon'
This is stuffed boned shoulder of lamb that is tied up to look like a balloon. To reassemble the shoulder, spread the stuffing on one half of the boned lamb and fold the other half close up over to cover it. If the shoulder has been tunnel-boned, push the stuffing into it. Turn the shoulder over, skinned side up. Tie the end of a 3m/9ft piece of string firmly round the shoulder, making a knot in the middle at the top. Take the string around again, but this time at right angles to the first line, again tying at the first knot. Continue this process until the 'balloon' is trussed about 8 times. Tuck in any loose flaps of meat or skin.

CLARET

Veal Medallions and Grilled Vegetables with Aïoli

Serves 8
8 × 140g/5oz veal medallions
olive oil
salt and freshly ground black pepper

For the aïoli
6 cloves of garlic, peeled and crushed
3 egg yolks
3 tablespoons fresh white breadcrumbs
$^{1}/_{2}$ teaspoon salt
4 tablespoons white wine vinegar
290ml/$^{1}/_{2}$ pint olive oil
1 tablespoon boiling water

For the vegetables
2 aubergines, cut in slices lengthways
olive oil
3 large red peppers, halved and deseeded
6 medium courgettes, cut into thin diagonal slices
4 onions, sliced
6 tomatoes, peeled, quartered and deseeded
balsamic vinegar
finely chopped fresh mint
finely chopped fresh basil

1. Make the aïoli: put the garlic, egg yolks, breadcrumbs, salt and vinegar into a food processor. Process to a paste, then with the motor running, slowly add the oil to make a thick sauce. Add the boiling water.
2. Salt the aubergines and leave in a colander for 20 minutes to extract the bitter juices (degorge). Rinse and pat dry with absorbent kitchen paper. Paint each side of the aubergine slices lightly with oil and grill until dark brown but not burnt.
3. Preheat the grill to its highest setting.
4. Grill the peppers skin side up until they are charred and blistered. Remove the skin and cut the flesh into strips.
5. Lightly oil the courgettes and grill until just cooked.
6. Sauté the onions in a little oil until light brown.
7. Layer the vegetables, including the tomatoes in a bowl, sprinkling each layer with balsamic vinegar, mint and basil. Set aside to marinate at room temperature for 1 hour.
8. Brush both sides of the veal with oil and sprinkle with salt and pepper. Grill under a preheated grill for 3–4 minutes each side, depending on the thickness of the meat.
9. To serve: place the cooked veal and some of the marinated vegetables on warmed dinner plates. Serve a spoonful of aïoli beside the vegetables.

LIGHT FRUITY RED

Peppered Calves' Liver Salade Tiède

Serves 4
340g/12oz calves' liver, skinned and sliced
2 tablespoons freshly ground black and white
    peppercorns
salt
30g/1oz butter
2 tablespoons walnut oil
4 tablespoons raspberry or sherry vinegar
4 handfuls of salad leaves: rocket, chicory,
    radicchio, frisée
30g/1oz pinenuts, toasted

1. Remove any large tubes from the slices of liver. Cut into finger-length pieces.
2. Put the peppercorns on to a plate and season with salt. Roll the liver in the peppercorns to give a light crust.
3. Heat the butter in a large frying pan and fry the liver a few pieces at a time for about 1 minute, or until lightly browned on the outside but still pink in the middle. Lift the liver on to a plate and continue frying until all the liver is cooked.
4. When the liver is cooked, add the oil and vinegar to the frying pan. Bring to the boil, scraping any sediment from the bottom of the pan, then remove from the heat.
5. Put the salad leaves into a large bowl, add the liver, pour over the dressing, toss together lightly and sprinkle with the pinenuts. Serve immediately.

NOTE: As liver toughens on standing, this dish is best cooked at the very last minute.

FRENCH COUNTRY WHITE OR RED

DESSERTS

Spring Mint Parfait

Serves 6
oil for greasing
170g/6oz granulated sugar
2 sprigs of fresh mint
thinly pared zest of 1 lemon
water
3 egg whites
380ml/^{2}/$_3$ pint double cream
190ml/^{1}/$_3$ pint Greek yoghurt
20g/^{3}/$_4$oz (a large handful) fresh mint leaves, finely
  shredded

To decorate
6 small sprigs of fresh mint
1 egg white
caster sugar

1. Prepare a 12.5cm/5in soufflé dish: wrap a double-thickness piece of greaseproof paper around the dish and secure with string or an elastic band, so that the paper comes 5cm/2in over the top of the dish. Lightly oil the inside edge of the paper.
2. Put the sugar, sprigs of mint and lemon zest into a heavy-based saucepan with enough water to cover. Bring slowly to the boil without stirring, then, when the sugar has dissolved, simmer for 5 minutes. Remove the mint and lemon zest and continue to boil the syrup to the firm ball stage (see note).
3. Meanwhile, whisk the egg whites in a clean bowl until they form stiff peaks (preferably using an electric hand whisk), and when the sugar syrup is just ready pour it on to the whites, whisking continuously and being careful not to let the hot sugar touch the beaters. Work as quickly as possible.
4. When all the syrup has been added, whisk hard until the mixture is stiff, shiny and absolutely stable. When the whisk is lifted the meringue should not flow at all.
5. Lightly whip the cream and fold it into the meringue mixture with the yoghurt and shredded mint. Pour into the prepared soufflé dish and freeze for 2 hours before serving.
6. Prepare the decoration: brush a very little egg white all over each sprig of mint and dip into the caster sugar. Arrange in a single layer on a baking sheet lined with silicone paper and leave to dry in a warm, dry place for 1 hour.
7. To serve: remove the greaseproof paper from the sides of the parfait and arrange the mint sprigs on top.

MOSCATO D'ASTI

Rhubarb Strudel

Serves 4
900g/2lb rhubarb
grated zest of 1 orange
3 tablespoons redcurrant jelly
4 pieces of stem ginger, finely chopped
30g/1oz caster sugar
4 sheets of filo pastry
55g/2oz butter, melted
55g/2oz ground rice

To decorate
icing sugar

To serve
1 quantity orange crème anglaise (see page 219)

1. Preheat the oven to 200°C/400°F/gas mark 6.
2. Cut the rhubarb into 1cm/½in chunks. Put into a saucepan with the orange zest, redcurrant jelly, stem ginger and caster sugar and cook over a low heat for 7–10 minutes, or until the rhubarb is soft. Taste for sweetness and add more sugar if necessary. Remove from the heat and allow to cool.
3. Lay the pieces of filo on a clean work surface, brush generously with butter and sprinkle with ground rice.
4. Pile the rhubarb mixture on one end of the filo and roll up like a Swiss roll. Brush the outside with melted butter. Bake in the preheated oven for 20–25 minutes, or until golden-brown. Remove from the oven and dust generously with icing sugar. Serve warm, with the orange crème anglaise handed separately.

SAUTERNES

Chocolate Meringue Torte

Serves 8–10
oil for greasing
225g/8oz almonds, toasted
225g/8oz good-quality dark chocolate
225g/8oz pitted dates
6 egg whites
30g/1oz caster sugar
225g/8oz soft light brown sugar, sifted
225g/8oz mascarpone

To serve
icing sugar
kumquat and date compote (see page 219)

1. Preheat the oven to 180°C/350°F/gas mark 4.
2. Line 2 × 20cm/8in moule-à-manqué tins with lightly oiled kitchen foil.
3. Put the almonds, chocolate and dates into a food processor and pulse on and off until they are roughly chopped. Set aside.
4. Whisk the egg whites until they form stiff peaks, then add the caster sugar and continue to whisk until shiny.
5. Add the brown sugar and chopped almond, chocolate and date mixture, folding the ingredients into the egg whites with a large metal spoon until they are just combined. Divide the mixture between the prepared tins and spread to flatten.
6. Bake the tortes towards the bottom of the preheated oven for 45 minutes. Remove from the oven and allow to cool in the tins.
7. When the meringues are cold, peel away the foil.
8. Place one meringue bottom side up on a board and spread with the mascarpone, then place the second meringue on top.
9. Dust the torte with icing sugar and serve with the compote handed separately.

SAUTERNES

Baked Nectarines with Mascarpone and Praline

Serves 4

4 small or 2 large ripe nectarines, halved and
   stoned
110g/4oz mascarpone or mild soft goat's cheese
4 teaspoons soft dark brown sugar
30g/1oz praline, not ground (see page 9)
8 × 17.5cm/7in square sheets of filo pastry
55g/2oz butter, melted

1. Preheat the oven to 200°C/400°F/gas mark 6.
2. Take a small slice off the bottom of one half of each nectarine so it sits easily on the surface without toppling over. If there isn't a very large dip left from where the stone lay, enlarge the hole a little by scraping out some of the flesh with a teaspoon. Place a large spoonful of mascarpone in the centre of each nectarine half, pressing it into the hole left by the stone. Sprinkle a teaspoon of the sugar over the mascarpone in each nectarine.
3. Break up the praline a little by crushing it with the end of a rolling pin and divide the pieces into 4, pressing a quarter of the praline into the mascarpone on each of the nectarine halves. Replace the other nectarine halves back on top. (If using large nectarines you won't need to do this.)
4. Lay one sheet of filo flat on a clean, dry work surface and brush quickly with melted butter. Place another sheet of filo on top and brush with more melted butter. Place a nectarine in the centre, with the mascarpone layer horizontal, and gather up the edges to form a parcel like a Dick Whittington sack. Repeat with the remaining nectarines.
5. Place the parcels on a greased baking sheet, brush the outsides with more melted butter and bake in the centre of the preheated oven for 20 minutes, or until golden-brown. Serve immediately.

RECIATO DI SOAVE

Individual Steamed Autumn Puddings

Serves 6
170g/6oz blackberries
1 cooking apple, peeled and diced
2 pears, peeled and diced
1 quince or medlar, peeled and diced
85g/3oz soft light brown sugar
5 tablespoons brandy or sloe gin
170g/6oz unsalted butter, softened
110g/4oz caster sugar, plus extra for dusting
grated zest of 1 orange
2 eggs, beaten
110g/4oz self-raising flour
a pinch of salt
1 teaspoon ground cinnamon
5 tablespoons milk

To serve
cinnamon crème anglaise (see page 219)

1. Make the topping: put all the fruit together into a saucepan with the sugar and brandy or sloe gin. Bring to the boil, then lower the heat and poach for 15–20 minutes, or until all the fruit is soft. Lift the fruit into a bowl with a slotted spoon and if necessary reduce the cooking liquid to a syrupy consistency, then stir into the fruit.
2. Meanwhile, generously grease 6 dariole or timbale moulds with 55g/2oz of the butter and sprinkle with caster sugar. Put a generous tablespoon of the fruit mixture at the bottom of each mould and set aside.
3. In a mixing bowl, cream the remaining butter and when very soft, add the sugar. Beat until light and fluffy. Add the orange zest.
4. Gradually add the eggs, beating very well after each addition.
5. Sift the flour with the salt and cinnamon and fold into the mixture.
6. Add enough milk to give a dropping consistency (the mixture should be just loose enough to drop from a spoon).
7. Divide the mixture between the moulds, cover with greaseproof paper and then with kitchen foil and tie securely with string, to prevent moisture entering the puddings.
8. Steam over continuously boiling water for 45 minutes, keeping a close eye on the water, so that it does not boil dry.
9. Turn out the moulds and serve with chilled cinnamon crème anglaise.

SAUTERNES

Baked Stuffed Quinces

Serves 4
4 large quinces
30g/1oz butter, melted
110g/4oz dried apricots, roughly chopped
4 dried figs, chopped
30g/1oz ground almonds
2 tablespoons soft light brown sugar
2 tablespoons clear honey
$1/2$ teaspoon ground cardamom
5 tablespoons water
5 tablespoons brandy or Calvados

To serve
mascarpone
amaretti biscuits (optional)

1. Preheat the oven to 190°C/375°F/gas mark 5.
2. Wash the quinces. Remove the cores with an apple corer. Using a sharp knife, cut a ring just through the skin around the middle of each quince. Place in an ovenproof dish.
3. Mix together the butter, chopped dried fruit, ground almonds, sugar, honey and cardamom. Pack this stuffing into the centre of each quince and pour over the water and brandy or Calvados. Cover with kitchen foil and bake in the preheated oven for 1–1$1/4$ hours, or until the quinces are soft all the way through when tested with a skewer.
4. Arrange the quinces in a serving dish and spoon around the cooking juices. Serve warm or chilled with the mascarpone and amaretti biscuits, if using, handed separately.

MONBAZILLAC

Seville Orange Syllabub with Nougatine

Serves 4
For the syllabub
3 tablespoons Grand Marnier
3 tablespoons Seville orange marmalade
grated zest and juice of 2 Seville oranges
150ml/$\frac{1}{4}$ pint double cream
290ml/$\frac{1}{2}$ pint mascarpone

For the nougatine
55g/2oz caster sugar
55g/2oz hazelnuts, toasted and skinned
oil for greasing

1. Mix together the Grand Marnier, marmalade, orange zest and juice.
2. Mix the cream with the mascarpone in a bowl and add the marmalade mixture. Pour into individual dishes and chill.
3. Meanwhile, make the nougatine: put the sugar into a small saucepan and heat gently, stirring occasionally, until a rich dark caramel colour. Add the hazelnuts and stir together. Turn on to a lightly oiled baking sheet and leave for 15 minutes to set.
4. When the nougatine has cooled, grind coarsely in a food processor or chop finely. Just before serving, sprinkle over the syllabubs.

AUSTRALIAN LIQUEUR MUSCAT

Chocolate Shortbread Torte with Sticky Cranberry Glaze

Serves 6
For the shortbread base
170g/6oz unsalted butter
85g/3oz caster sugar
30g/1oz cocoa powder
225g/8oz plain flour

For the filling
225g/8oz full fat cream cheese
5 tablespoons double cream
140g/5oz plain chocolate

2 eggs
1 egg yolk
1 teaspoon coffee essence
2 tablespoons rum

For the topping
85g/3oz granulated sugar
5 tablespoons water
170g/6oz cranberries
5 tablespoons soured cream
icing sugar for dusting

1. Preheat the oven to 190°C/375°F/gas mark 5.
2. Make the shortbread base: melt the butter in a saucepan and stir in the sugar and cocoa powder. Remove from the heat and allow to cool for 2 minutes. Sift the flour and mix into the cooled butter mixture. Press the mixture on to the bottom of a 20cm/8in spring-form mould.
3. Bake in the preheated oven for 20–25 minutes, then remove from the oven and allow to cool for 5 minutes. Reduce the oven temperature to 150°C/300°F/gas mark 2.
4. Make the filling: beat the cream cheese until smooth.
5. Heat the cream and chocolate together in a small saucepan over a low heat until just melted. Stir into the cream cheese with the eggs, egg yolk, coffee essence and rum. Beat well until smooth and pour on to the cooled crust.
6. Return to the middle of the oven and bake for about 30 minutes, or until the filling has set. Remove from the oven and allow to cool.
7. Meanwhile, make the topping: heat the sugar and water together in a saucepan until dissolved. Add the cranberries and bring to the boil, then lower the heat and simmer for 5–7 minutes, or until the liquid has reduced to a glaze. Remove from the heat and allow to cool.
8. Spread the soured cream over the top of the torte and arrange the cranberries on top. Dust with icing sugar and serve.

SAUTERNES

Three Chocolate Bavarois

6 tablespoons water
15g/$\frac{1}{2}$oz powdered gelatine
375ml/13fl oz milk
8 egg yolks, beaten
45g/1$\frac{1}{2}$oz caster sugar
140g/5oz white chocolate, grated
140g/5oz milk chocolate, grated
140g/5oz plain chocolate, grated
720ml/1$\frac{1}{4}$ pints double cream, lightly whipped

To decorate
290ml/$\frac{1}{2}$ pint crème anglaise, flavoured with
    grated orange zest and/or 1 tablespoon Grand
    Marnier

1. Line a 900g/2lb loaf tin with a piece of greaseproof paper cut to fit the bottom of the tin. Lightly oil the tin.
2. Place the water in a small saucepan and sprinkle over the gelatine. Leave for 5 minutes to become spongy.
3. Bring the milk to the boil in a saucepan. Beat the eggs and sugar together with a wooden spoon and pour over the milk. Return the mixture to the saucepan and heat gently, stirring constantly with a wooden spoon until the custard will coat the back of the spoon.
4. Place each variety of chocolate in a separate bowl and divide the custard equally between them, pouring through a sieve to remove any egg threads. Stir well to melt the chocolate.
5. Dissolve the gelatine over a low heat without boiling until liquid and clear, then add half to the white chocolate custard. Stir gently and when the mixture is on the point of setting, fold in one-third of the cream. Pour into the base of the loaf tin. Refrigerate until set.
6. Once the white chocolate bavarois has set, reheat the remaining gelatine without boiling, and add half of it to the milk chocolate custard. When it is on the point of setting, fold in another third of the cream. Pour over the set white chocolate bavarois, very carefully. Refrigerate until set.
7. Once the milk chocolate bavarois has set, reheat the remaining gelatine without boiling and add it to the plain chocolate custard. When it is on the point of setting, fold in the remaining cream. Pour very carefully over the set milk chocolate bavarois and refrigerate until set.
8. To serve: turn the bavarois out carefully, using a knife to loosen it, or dip the tin very quickly in boiling water. Remove the greaseproof paper from the top. Slice the bavarois with a hot knife and serve with the flavoured crème anglaise.

FORTIFIED SWEET WHITE

Ballymaloe's Jelly of Fresh Raspberries with a Mint Cream

Sally Procter of Leith's spent a happy few days at Ballymaloe cookery school run by Dorina Allen in Ireland and came back with several excellent recipes. This is a particularly delicious pudding for the summer.

Serves 6
560g/1¹/₄lb fresh raspberries
225g/8oz caster sugar
290ml/¹/₂ pint water
4 sprigs of fresh mint
2 teaspoons Framboise liqueur
1 tablespoon lemon juice
3 tablespoons water
1 tablespoon powdered gelatine

For the mint cream
15 fresh mint leaves
1 tablespoon lemon juice
200ml/7fl oz double cream

To decorate
fresh mint leaves

1. Pick over the raspberries and reserve about 110g/4oz of the best ones for decoration.
2. Put the sugar, water and mint sprigs into a small, heavy saucepan. Bring slowly to the boil. Simmer for a few minutes, then remove from the heat and allow to cool. Add the Framboise and lemon juice.
3. Put the 3 tablespoons water into a small saucepan and sprinkle over the gelatine. Leave for 5 minutes to become spongy.
4. Oil 6 ramekins very lightly.
5. Strain the flavoured syrup into a bowl. Dissolve the gelatine over a low heat without boiling until liquid and clear, then add it to the strained syrup. Add the raspberries.
6. Pour three-quarters of the jelly into the ramekins, making sure that all the raspberries are used up. Refrigerate until beginning to set, then spoon over the remaining jelly. (This is to ensure that the jellies have flat bottoms when turned out.)
7. Meanwhile, make the mint cream: crush the mint leaves in a pestle and mortar with the lemon juice. Add the cream and stir. The lemon juice will thicken the cream. If the cream becomes too thick, add a little water.
8. Divide the mint cream between 6 pudding plates and spread it over the surface of each. Turn out a raspberry jelly on top of the cream in the centre of the plate. Decorate with the reserved raspberries and extra mint leaves.

LIGHT SWEET WHITE

Charlotte's Higgledy Piggledy Tart

Serves 8–10

225g/8oz flour quantity Martha Stewart's walnut
    pastry (see page 218)
150ml/¼ pint double cream, lightly whipped
290ml/½ pint crème pâtissière (see page 219)
soft seasonal fruit, such as apricots, oranges,
    plums, kiwis, bananas and strawberries
warm apricot glaze (see page 220)

1. Line a 25cm/10in flan ring with the pastry, pressing it in. Refrigerate for 30 minutes.
2. Preheat the oven to 190°C/375°F/gas mark 5.
3. Bake the flan case blind (see page 7). Leave to cool.
4. Fold the cream into the almost cold crème pâtissière and pile into the flan case. Spread out evenly.
5. Prepare the fruit as for a fruit salad and arrange in a higgledy piggledy fashion in the flan case.
6. Brush or spoon the warm apricot glaze over the top.

SWEET WHITE

Poached Pear and Polenta Tart with Soft Cream

Serves 8
425ml/3/4 pint red wine
55g/2oz sugar
6 whole cloves
3 strips of thinly pared lemon zest
1/2 teaspoon ground cinnamon
8 pears

For the pastry
140g/5oz butter at room temperature
140g/5oz sugar

3 egg yolks
200g/7oz plain flour
85g/3oz polenta, plus 1 tablespoon
1/2 teaspoon salt

For the soft cream
150ml/1/4 pint double cream
pear poaching liquid (see recipe)
brandy to taste
a few drops of vanilla essence

1. Bring the wine, sugar, cloves, lemon zest and cinnamon to the boil in a medium saucepan and simmer until reduced by about one-fifth.
2. Peel the pears and cut them in half. Remove the cores carefully with an apple corer. Cut the pears into 1cm/1/2in slices. Put the pear slices into the wine mixture and cook carefully over a low heat for about 40 minutes, or until the pears are tender. Lift them out with a slotted spoon and allow them to cool to room temperature.
3. Strain the wine to remove the lemon zest and cloves. Put the syrup back on the heat, bring to the boil and reduce by half. Some of this will be used to flavour the cream. Preheat the oven to 200°C/400°F/gas mark 6.
4. Make the pastry: cream the butter and sugar together until well blended. Add the egg yolks one at a time, beating well after each addition. Sift the flour, 85g/3oz polenta and salt together and mix into the creamed mixture. Beat until the dough comes together, then knead lightly on a floured surface, adding more flour if necessary, until the pastry is no longer sticky. Refrigerate for 20 minutes.
5. Cut the dough in half. Press one half of the dough on to the base and sides of a 22cm/9in flan ring. Sprinkle the base with the tablespoon of polenta. Spoon the drained pears into the pastry case.
6. Roll out the remaining dough 1cm/1/2in thick. Using a fluted biscuit cutter, cut out as many circles as possible from the dough. Place them on top of the pears, starting on the outside. Overlap the shapes and continue to cover the top.
7. Bake the tart in the preheated oven for about 30 minutes, covering with greaseproof paper after 20 minutes if the tart shows signs of becoming too dark.
8. Make the soft cream: whip the double cream until soft peaks are formed. Flavour with some of the poaching liquid, the brandy and the vanilla essence to taste. Serve with the warm tart.

SWEET WHITE

Individual Apple Tarts with Calvados Crème Anglaise

Serves 4
225g/8oz flour quantity puff pastry (see page 217)
4 dessert apples
caster sugar
beaten egg, to glaze
warm apricot glaze (see page 220)

To serve
1 tablespoon Calvados
290ml/$\frac{1}{2}$ pint crème anglaise (see page 219)

1. Preheat the oven to 200°C/400°F/gas mark 6.
2. Roll out the pastry 2mm/$\frac{1}{8}$in thick and cut into 4 circles 12.5cm/5in in diameter. Place on a damp baking sheet. Using a sharp knife, trace an inner circle about 1cm/$\frac{1}{2}$in from the edge of each pastry circle. Do not cut all the way through the pastry.
3. Peel, core and thinly slice the apples and arrange in concentric circles within the border of each pastry tart. Using a sharp knife, mark a pattern on the pastry border.
4. Sprinkle lightly with caster sugar. Brush the rim of each pastry circle with beaten egg, taking care not to let it drop down the sides of the pastry.
5. Flour the blade of a knife and use this to knock up the sides of the pastry. Refrigerate for 15 minutes.
6. Bake in the preheated oven for 20 minutes. Remove from the oven and leave to cool slightly, then brush liberally with warm apricot glaze.
7. Add the Calvados to the well-chilled crème anglaise. Serve the tarts warm with the cold custard.

SWEET WHITE

Gâteau Pithiviers

Serves 6
225g/8oz flour quantity puff pastry (see page 217)
1 egg, beaten, with ¹/₂ teaspoon salt
icing sugar

For the almond filling
125g/4¹/₂oz butter, softened
125g/4¹/₂oz sugar
1 egg
1 egg yolk
125g/4¹/₂oz whole blanched almonds, skinned
  and ground
15g/¹/₂oz plain flour
2 tablespoons rum

1. Refrigerate the puff pastry.
2. Make the almond filling: cream the butter in a bowl, add the sugar and beat thoroughly. Beat in the egg and the egg yolk; then stir in the ground almonds, flour and rum.
3. Roll out half the puff pastry to a circle about 27cm/11in in diameter. Using a pan lid as a guide, cut out a 25cm/10in circle from this with a sharp knife, angling the knife slightly. Roll out the remaining pastry slightly thicker than for the first round and cut out another 25cm/10in circle. Set the thinner circle on a baking sheet, mound the filling in the centre, leaving a 2.5cm/1in border, and brush the border with beaten egg. Set the second circle on top and press the edges together firmly.
4. Scallop the edge of the gâteau by pulling it in at intervals with the back of a knife. Brush the gâteau with beaten egg, and, working from the centre, score the top in curves like the petals of a flower. Do not cut through to the filling. Refrigerate the gâteau for 15–20 minutes. Preheat the oven to 220°C/425°F/gas mark 7.
5. Bake the gâteau in the oven for 30–35 minutes, or until firm, puffed and brown.
6. Preheat the grill to its highest setting.
7. Dust the gâteau with icing sugar. Place under the grill until lightly glazed.

SWEET SPARKLING WHITE

Sablé aux Fraises

This recipe has been adapted from *The Roux Brothers on Pâtisserie*.

Serves 6
280g/10oz flour quantity pâte sablée (see page
   219)
675g/1½lb strawberries, hulled and sliced
425ml/¾ pint raspberry coulis (see page 220)
55g/2oz icing sugar, sifted, for dusting

1. Preheat the oven to 190°C/375°F/gas mark 5.
2. Divide the chilled dough into 2 pieces to make for easier rolling.
3. Roll out the doughs very thinly and cut into a total of 18 × 10cm/4in circles. Refrigerate to relax for 10 minutes. Bake in the preheated oven for 8 minutes or until pale golden. Transfer to a wire rack and leave to cool.
4. Cut the strawberries in half and mix them with two-thirds of the raspberry coulis. Leave to macerate.
5. Place a pastry base on each of 6 pudding plates. Arrange a few macerated strawberries on top. Cover with a second pastry base and more strawberries. Cover with a third piece of pastry and dust generously with icing sugar.
6. Serve the remaining raspberry coulis separately or poured around the sablés.

NOTE: Do not assemble the puddings in advance as the pastry will become soggy.

Lemon Curd Ice Cream

Serves 6
4 egg yolks
grated zest and juice of 2 lemons
125g/4½oz caster sugar
110g/4oz unsalted butter, at room temperature,
   cut into small pieces
570ml/1 pint plain yoghurt

1. Put the egg yolks, lemon zest and juice, sugar and butter into a small saucepan. Set over a low heat and stir with a wooden spoon until the butter has melted and the curd is thick enough to coat the back of the spoon.
2. Remove from the heat and allow the curd to cool, then stir in the yoghurt. Cover closely and freeze.
3. Transfer the ice cream to the refrigerator about an hour before serving.

NOTE: This ice cream is also delicious made with good-quality shop-bought lemon curd.

Brandy Snap Tortes

Serves 6
110g/4oz flour quantity brandy snap mixture (see
   page 218)
450g/1lb damson ice cream, slightly softened (see
   below)
raspberry coulis (see page 220)
100g/4oz mixed raspberries and blueberries

To decorate
sprigs of fresh mint
icing sugar, sifted, for dusting

1. Preheat the oven to 190°C/375°F/ gas mark 5. Line a baking sheet with non-stick baking parchment. Grease a palette knife.
2. Make the brandy snap mixture, adding the extra 1 teaspoon ground ginger. Bake 18 brandy snaps on the baking sheet as in the recipe on page 218 but lift them, flat, on to a wire rack and leave them to cool and harden.
3. Put a flat brandy snap on to each of 6 pudding plates. Cover with some of the damson ice cream and flatten slightly. Cover with a second flat brandy snap. Arrange some more ice cream on top of the brandy snaps and cover with a third brandy snap.
4. Pour the raspberry coulis around the tortes.
5. Arrange the raspberries and blueberries on the coulis and decorate with a small sprig of mint.
6. Dust lightly with icing sugar.

DAMSON ICE CREAM
Serves 6–8
450g/1lb damsons
340g/12oz caster sugar
150ml/$\frac{1}{4}$ pint water
2 large egg whites
juice and finely grated rind of 1 small orange
290ml/$\frac{1}{2}$ pint double cream

1. Wash the damsons and put them, still wet, with 110g/4oz of the sugar in a thick-bottomed saucepan. Stew gently, covered, over very gentle heat or bake in the oven until soft and pulpy.
2. Push through a sieve, removing the stones.
3. Dissolve the remaining 225g/8oz sugar in the water and bring to the boil.
4. Boil steadily for 5 minutes.
5. While the syrup is boiling, beat the egg whites in an electric mixer or by hand until stiff. Pour the boiling syrup on to the egg whites, whisking as you do so. The mixture will go rather liquid at this stage, but keep whisking until you have a thick meringue.
6. Stir in the orange rind and juice and the purée.
7. Whip the cream until thick but not solid, and fold it into the mixture.
8. Freeze. It is not necessary to re-whisk the ice cream during freezing.

NOTE: The damson purée can be replayced by a purée of cooked plums, greengages, rhubarb, dried apricots or prunes, or a raw purée of soft fruit, such as fresh apricots or peaches.

Frozen Raspberry Yoghurt

Quick, simple and delicious, this recipe can also be made using strawberries.

Serves 6
450g/1lb raspberries
110g/4oz icing sugar
425ml/³/₄ pint Greek yoghurt
2 egg whites
3 tablespoons caster sugar

1. Process half the raspberries and pass through a sieve to make a purée. In a large bowl, mix the raspberry purée with the icing sugar and yoghurt until thoroughly blended. Cover and chill in the refrigerator for 30 minutes.
2. In a medium bowl, whisk the egg whites to medium peaks. Add the caster sugar and continue whisking until shiny and stiff.
3. Gently fold the raspberry yoghurt mixture into the meringue until well combined. Pour into a freezer-proof container and freeze the mixture for about 3 hours, until solid but still soft enough to give when pressed with a finger.
4. Tip the ice cream into a chilled bowl and break it up with a fork, then process or whisk until smooth and pale. Gently mix in the remaining raspberries and freeze again.
5. Transfer the frozen yoghurt to the refrigerator 20 minutes before serving. Serve with warm chocolate sauce.

NOTE: Ice creams made with yoghurt inevitably have a crystal-like texture. The more they are whisked, the smoother they become. If you have an ice-cream machine, however, they will be almost as smooth as other ice creams.

AUSTRALIAN LIQUEUR MUSCAT

Marmalade Pudding

Serves 2
butter for greasing
1 orange
1 tablespoon orange marmalade
knob of butter
55g/2oz soft butter
55g/2oz caster sugar
55g/2oz self-raising flour
1 egg

To serve
Crème anglaise (see page 219)

1. Grease a 570ml/1 pint ovenproof dish. Using a sharp knife, peel the orange as you would an apple, removing all the pith and peel and saving any juice. Cut the orange into slices, discarding any pips. Arrange the slices in an overlapping layer in the prepared dish.
2. Put the marmalade into a small saucepan with the knob of butter. Place over the heat and stir until boiling. Pour over the orange slices.
3. Set the oven to 190°C/375°F/gas mark 5. Put the butter, sugar, flour and egg into a mixing bowl with the reserved orange juice. Beat until light and fluffy. Spread on top of the marmalade base.
4. Bake for about 30 minutes until golden-brown and firm when pressed with the fingertips. Loosen round the edges with a knife and turn on to a serving dish. Serve crème anglaise.

Grilled Berry Meringue

Serves 2
85g/3oz frozen summer fruit
2 tablespoons apple juice
1 teaspoon sherry
2 trifle sponges
150ml/$\frac{1}{4}$ pint double cream
1 egg white
55g/2oz caster sugar

1. Place the frozen fruit in a bowl, spoon the apple juice and sherry over it and leave to defrost. Arrange the trifle sponges in the base of a 570ml/1 pint soufflé dish and add the defrosted fruit and all the juice.
2. Whip the cream lightly and spread over the fruit.
3. Heat the grill to high. Whisk the egg white until stiff. Add half the sugar and continue to whisk until very stiff and shiny. Fold in the remaining sugar.
4. Spread the meringue over the whipped cream, leaving a rough surface. Grill for a few minutes until browned on top. (This happens quickly, so keep watching.) Allow to cool before serving.

Citrus Fruit Compote with Spiced Caramel

Serves 6
3 large oranges
1 pink grapefruit
6 kumquats
1 small pineapple

For the spiced caramel
225g/8oz granulated sugar
290ml/$\frac{1}{2}$ pint water
2 bay leaves
2 star anise
1 cinnamon stick
1 tablespoon coriander seeds, crushed
1 strip of lemon zest
2.5cm/1in piece of fresh root ginger, peeled and
    roughly chopped

1. Make the spiced caramel: put the sugar and half the water into a heavy-bottomed saucepan and dissolve the sugar slowly without boiling. When the sugar has dissolved, turn up the heat and boil until the melted sugar is a dark caramel colour.
2. Remove from the heat immediately and pour in the remaining water, taking care as the mixture can spit. Add the remaining caramel ingredients to the pan and leave to cool, preferably overnight.
3. Prepare the fruit: peel, removing all pith, and segment the oranges and grapefruit. Slice the kumquats very thinly.
4. Peel and core the pineapple and cut into chunks. Put the fruit into a serving bowl, then strain over the caramel. Chill well before serving.

Baked Exotic Fruits

Serves 6
400ml/14oz tin lychees, drained and juice reserved
1 mango, peeled and sliced
20 strawberries, hulled
110g/4oz blueberries
110g/4oz raspberries
pulp and juice of 8 passion-fruit
grated zest of 1 lime
2 tablespoons kirsch (optional)

For the syrup
1 clove
grated zest and juice of 1 lime
1 vanilla pod, split open
1 cm/$\frac{1}{2}$ inch fresh ginger, grated
1 sprig rosemary
1 star anise

1. Set the oven to 240°C/475°F/gas mark 8.
2. Mix the fruit and lime zest together carefully, place in an ovenproof dish and set aside.
3. Bring the lychee juice and syrup ingredients to the boil and reduce, by boiling rapidly, to a syrupy consistency.
4. Pour the syrup over the fruits, drizzle with the kirsch (if using), cover with a lid or foil and bake for 7 minutes. Serve hot.

Chocolate Profiteroles

These look spectacular piled high in a pyramid on the serving dish.

Makes 30

For the profiteroles
1 quantity choux pastry (see page 217)

For the filling and topping
570ml/1 pint double cream, whipped and
    sweetened with 1 tablespoon sifted icing sugar
110g/4oz plain chocolate, chopped
15g/½oz butter
2 tablespoons water

1. Preheat the oven to 200°C/400°F/gas mark 6.
2. Put teaspoons of the choux mixture on a baking sheet, about 7.5cm/3in apart.
3. Bake in the preheated oven for 20–30 minutes. The profiteroles will puff up and become fairly brown. If they are taken out when only slightly brown, they will be soggy when cool.
4. Using a skewer, make a hole the size of a pea in the base of each profiterole and return to the oven for 5 minutes to allow the insides to dry out. Leave to cool completely on a wire rack.
5. When cold, put the sweetened cream into a piping bag fitted with a small plain nozzle. Pipe the cream into the profiteroles through the holes made by the skewer, until well filled.
6. Put the chocolate, butter and water in a heatproof bowl set over (not in) a saucepan of simmering water and leave until melted.
7. Dip the tops of the profiteroles in the melted chocolate, then allow to cool.

NOTE: If no piping bag is available for filling the profiteroles, they can be split, allowed to dry out, and filled with cream or crème pâtissière (see page 219) when cold, and the icing can be spooned over the top. However, made this way they are messier to eat with the fingers.

AUSTRALIAN LIQUEUR MUSCAT

Mince Pies

Makes 20–24 tarts
340g/12oz flour quantity well-chilled rich
    shortcrust pastry (see page 218)
450g/1lb mincemeat (see page 218)

To glaze
beaten egg or milk

To serve
icing sugar

1. Set the oven to 190°C/375°F/gas mark 5.
2. Divide the pastry in half and roll one half out thinly and use it to line tartlet tins.
3. Fill each tartlet tin with enough mincemeat to come about three-quarters of the way up the pastry.
4. Roll out the remaining pastry and either stamp into shapes, such as stars, dampen lightly with water and press firmly but gently on top of the mincemeat or cut into circles to fit the tarts as lids. Dampen the pastry edges and press the tops down lightly, sealing the edges carefully.
5. Brush your chosen glaze on the lids – the milk will give a matt finish, and the beaten egg a shiny finish.
6. Snip the lids with a pair of scissors or a sharp knife to make a small slit for the steam to escape, leaving the shapes untouched.
7. Bake for 20 minutes until light golden brown.
8. Cool on a wire rack.
9. Serve warm sprinkled with icing sugar.

NOTE: Once completely cold, mince pies can be frozen or stored in an airtight container.

LIQUEUR MUSCAT SUCH AS BEAUMES DE VENISE

Creamed Cheese with Fresh Fruit

Serves 4–6
225g/8oz cottage cheese
290ml/$\frac{1}{2}$ pint double cream, lightly whipped
55g/2oz icing sugar, sifted
2 drops vanilla essence
3 figs, quartered
3 kiwis, peeled and sliced
4 oranges, peeled and segmented

1. Put the cottage cheese into a sieve and drain very well.
2. Push the cheese through the sieve (or process briefly in a processor) and fold in the lightly whipped double cream. Sweeten with icing sugar and add the vanilla essence.
3. Pile on to a large oval dish and shape into a shallow mound. Arrange the fruit attractively on top of the cheese.

LIGHT SWEET WINE

Tarte Tatin

Serves 6
For the pastry
170g/6oz plain flour
55g/2oz ground rice
140g/5oz butter
55g/2oz caster sugar
1 egg, beaten

For the topping
110g/4oz butter
110g/4oz granulated sugar
900g/2lb cooking apples
grated rind of 1 lemon

1. Set the oven to 190°C/375°F/gas mark 5.
2. To make the pastry: sift the flour and ground rice into a large bowl. Rub in the butter until the mixture resembles breadcrumbs. Stir in the sugar. Add the egg and bind the dough together. Chill while you prepare the top.
3. To make the topping: melt the butter in a 25cm/10in frying pan with a metal handle. Add the granulated sugar and remove from the heat. Peel, core and thickly slice the apples. Arrange the apple slices over the melted butter and sugar in the base of the frying pan. Sprinkle the grated lemon rind over the top.
4. Place the frying pan over a high flame until the butter and sugar start to caramelize. It may take 6–7 minutes and you will be able to smell the change – it is essential that the apples get dark. Remove from the heat.
5. Roll the pastry into a circle, 5mm/$\frac{1}{4}$in thick, to fit the top of the pan. Lay it on top of the apples and press down lightly. Bake in the oven for 25–30 minutes.
6. Allow to cool slightly, turn out on to a plate and serve warm.

NOTE: If you do not have a frying pan with a metal handle, cook the apples in an ordinary frying pan. Let the butter and sugar become well caramelized and tip into an ovenproof dish. Cover with the pastry and then bake in the oven on a hot baking sheet. It can also be made in a shallow cast-iron dish – if it has handles (or flanges) turning out the Tarte Tatin is quite difficult, but not impossible.

SWEET WHITE

Pistachio Parfait

Serves 6
225g/8oz caster sugar
60ml/2½fl oz water
3 egg whites
570ml/1 pint double cream
few drops of green colouring
15ml/1 tablespoon vanilla essence
5ml/1 teaspoon almond essence
75g/2½ pistachio nuts, chopped

1. Put the sugar and water in a heavy saucepan.
2. Without stirring, bring it slowly to the boil.
3. Boil until the syrup will form a thread when dropped from a spoon.
4. While the syrup is gently boiling at the correct stage, whisk the egg whites to stiff peaks.
5. If the whites are in a machine, pour the bubbling syrup on to them in a steady stream while whisking, taking care not to pour the syrup on to the wires of the whisk – it cools fast against the cold metal and can harden and stick to the whisk. If whisking the whites by hand, and in the absence of anyone to pour while you whisk, pour the syrup on to the whites in stages, about one-third at a time, whisking hard between each addition, and working as fast as possible. The styrup must be bubbling hot as it hits the egg white to partially cook it.
6. When all the syrup has been added, whisk hard until the mixture is stiff and shiny and absolutely stable. If the whisk is lifted, the meringue should not flow at all.
7. Lightly whip the cream and colour it a delicate green.
8. Fold the cream into the meringue mixture. Add the essences and chopped nuts.
9. Freeze and remove from the freezer half an hour before serving.

NOTE: This recipe also works well with pears; cook them for 20 minutes.

CAKES, PASTRIES AND BREADS

Squashy Rhubarb Cake

This cake can also be served as a winter pudding, to serve 4, accompanied by crème anglaise or double cream.

For the crumble topping
55g/2oz butter
85g/3oz plain flour
30g/1oz sugar

For the cake
melted lard or oil for greasing tin
85g/3oz butter
85g/3oz sugar
2 small eggs, beaten
85g/3oz self-raising flour, sifted with a pinch of salt
milk

For the filling
675g/1½lb rhubarb, cut into 2.5cm/1in pieces
1 tablespoon sugar

To finish
icing sugar, sifted

1. Preheat the oven to 190°C/375°F/gas mark 5. Grease a 20cm/8in loose-bottomed cake tin.
2. Make the crumble topping: rub the butter into the flour in a bowl and add the sugar. Set aside.
3. Make the cake: cream the butter in a mixing bowl until soft. Add the sugar and cream until very pale, light and fluffy.
4. Add the eggs gradually to the mixture, beating well after each addition. Add a spoonful of the flour if necessary, to prevent the mixture from curdling.
5. Fold in the flour, using a large metal spoon, and add a few dribbles of milk if necessary, to achieve a reluctant dropping consistency.
6. Turn into the prepared tin and spread out evenly flat. Cover carefully with the rhubarb pieces tossed in the sugar. Sprinkle with the crumble mixture.
7. Bake in the centre of the oven for about 45 minutes or until the top feels firm to the touch.
8. Remove the cake from the oven and allow to cool completely in the tin before turning out.
9. Just before serving, remove the cake from the tin and dust with icing sugar.

NOTE: Tinned rhubarb may be used, without the sugar. You will need a 450g/1lb tin, drained.

Chocolate Polenta Cake

This delicious cake can also be served as a pudding and is perfect with fresh raspberries and Greek yoghurt or crème fraîche.

melted lard or oil for greasing tin
225g/8oz plain chocolate, chopped
110g/4oz unsalted butter
5 eggs
140g/5oz caster sugar
3 tablespoons dark rum
85g/3oz fine polenta

1. Preheat the oven to 180°C/350°F/gas mark 4. Grease a 20cm/8in moule-à-manqué tin or a 22cm/9in sandwich tin. Line the base with a disc of greased greaseproof paper. Dust lightly with caster sugar and then flour. Tap out the excess.
2. Put the chocolate into a saucepan with the butter. Melt gently over a low heat. Remove from the heat and allow to cool slightly in a bowl.
3. Separate the eggs. Beat the yolks with 85g/3oz of the sugar. Add 1 tablespoon of the rum and continue beating until thick and pale.
4. Fold the melted chocolate mixture into the egg and sugar mixture.
5. Whisk the egg whites until thick and holding a medium peak. Gradually whisk in the remaining sugar until thick and glossy.
6. Fold the remaining rum and the polenta into the chocolate mixture, using a large metal spoon, and finally fold in the egg whites. Pour into the prepared tin.
7. Bake in the centre of the oven for 40–50 minutes or until a sharp knife or skewer inserted into the centre comes out clean.
8. Remove the cake from the oven and allow to cool in the tin for 10 minutes, then turn out on to a serving plate and leave to cool completely.

NOTE: The cake is turned directly on to a plate as it is fragile and can break if it is moved.

Old-fashioned Boiled Christmas Cake

This cake is not, as the name suggests, boiled instead of baked, but the fruit is boiled in water and orange juice and allowed to stand for 3 days before completing. This gives the fruit a wonderful plumpness. Instead of being decorated with marzipan and icing it is finished with a glazed fruit and nut topping and a pretty ribbon.

225g/8oz sultanas
225g/8oz raisins
110g/4oz currants
55g/2oz mixed peel
55g/2oz glacé cherries, halved
170g/6oz dried apricots, chopped
55g/2oz dried apples, chopped
110g/4oz dried dates, chopped
110g/4oz dried peaches, chopped
110g/4oz dried pears, chopped
225g/8oz butter
225g/8oz brown sugar
grated rind and juice of 1 lemon
grated rind and juice of 1 orange
110ml/4fl oz water
110ml/4fl oz orange juice
110ml/4fl oz brandy

2.5ml/$\frac{1}{2}$ teaspoon grated nutmeg
5ml/1 teaspoon ground cinnamon
5ml/1 teaspoon allspice
2.5ml/$\frac{1}{2}$ teaspoon ground ginger
1.25ml/$\frac{1}{4}$ teaspoon ground cardamom
15ml/1 tablespoon black treacle
5 eggs, beaten
310g/11oz plain flour
5ml/1 teaspoon baking powder

For the fruit topping
340g/12oz mixed dried fruit and nuts, e.g. pecans, brazils, almonds, apricots, red and green cherries, prunes, peaches, pears etc.
340g/12oz apricot jam

1. Put the sultanas, raisins, currants, mixed peel, cherries, apricots, apples, dates, peaches, pears, butter, sugar, lemon and orange rind and juice, water and orange juice into a large pan. Bring slowly to the boil. Stir with a wooden spoon, cover with a lid, and simmer for 10 minutes.
2. Remove from the heat and allow to cool slightly. Add the brandy and spices and transfer to a large bowl. When it is completely cold, cover and put in a cool place (not the refrigerator) for 3 days, stirring daily.
3. Prepare a 25cm/10in round cake tin by lining with double sheets of greaseproof paper. Preheat the oven to 170°C/325°F/gas mark 3.
4. Stir the treacle into the boiled fruit mixture and beat in the eggs. Sift together the flour and baking powder and stir into the cake mixture, which will be slightly sloppy. Turn it into the prepared cake tin and bake for approximately 4$\frac{1}{2}$ hours, or until a skewer inserted into the centre of the cake comes out clean.
5. Leave to cool in the tin.
6. When completely cold, wrap up carefully in aluminium foil until ready to decorate. It will mature well for 2–3 months.
7. To decorate the cake: put the apricot jam in a pan with 15ml/1 tablespoon of water. Heat until boiling and then push through a sieve. Allow to cool slightly and then brush the top of the cake with the apricot glaze. Arrange the fruit and nuts all over the top of the cake in a haphazard fashion and then, using a pastry brush, glaze carefully with the apricot glaze.

Saffron Cake

Saffron cake is particularly popular in Cornwall. This is because the Phoenicians traded saffron for Cornish tin. Nowadays saffron is so expensive that saffron cakes sold in bakeries usually contain only a very little saffron and are coloured with yellow food dye. Only cakes labelled 'genuine saffron cake' contain the real thing.

30 saffron strands
150ml/5fl oz boiling water
15g/^{1}/$_2$oz fresh yeast
110g/4oz caster sugar
85ml/3fl oz lukewarm milk
450g/1lb plain flour
^{1}/$_2$ teaspoon salt
^{1}/$_4$ teaspoon freshly grated nutmeg
^{1}/$_4$ teaspoon ground cinnamon
85g/3oz butter
85g/3oz lard
melted lard for greasing tin
110g/4oz sultanas
110g/4oz currants
30g/1oz mixed peel

To glaze
beaten egg

1. Soak the strands of saffron in the boiling water for about 2 hours.
2. Cream the yeast with 1 teaspoon of the sugar and add the milk.
3. Sift the flour, salt and spices together into a large mixing bowl. Cut the butter and lard into pieces and rub in with the fingertips.
4. Make a well in the centre and add the yeast mixture, saffron and saffron-flavoured water. Mix to a soft dough, first with a round-bladed knife and then with the fingers of one hand. Knead well until the dough is smooth and elastic. Place in a large clean bowl, cover with greased clingfilm or a clean damp cloth, and leave in a warm place to rise until doubled in bulk.
5. Preheat the oven to 190°C/375°F/gas mark 5 and grease a 900g/2lb loaf tin.
6. Take the risen dough out of the bowl, scatter over the remaining sugar and the dried fruit and peel. Knock back the dough and knead in the fruit, distributing evenly throughout the dough.
7. Shape into a loaf and put into the prepared tin. Cover, return to the warm place and leave until 1^1/$_2$ times its original bulk. This will take about 15 minutes, depending on the warmth of the room.
8. Glaze the top of the loaf with beaten egg and bake in the oven for 20 minutes, then turn the oven temperature down to 180°C/350°F/gas mark 4 and bake for 25 further minutes or until the cake sounds hollow when tapped on the underside.
9. Turn out on to a wire rack and leave to cool completely.

Orange and Poppy Seed Cake

melted lard or oil for greasing tin
110g/4oz butter
225g/8oz sugar
4 eggs, beaten
225g/8oz plain flour
2$\frac{1}{2}$ teaspoons baking powder
150ml/5fl oz milk
85g/3oz poppy seeds
1 teaspoon vanilla essence
finely grated zest of 2 oranges

For the glaze
110ml/4fl oz fresh orange juice
110g/4oz granulated sugar

1. Preheat the oven to 160°C/325°F/gas mark 3. Grease a 23cm/9$\frac{1}{2}$in loose-bottomed cake tin and line the base with a disc of greased greaseproof paper.
2. Cream the butter and sugar together in a mixing bowl until light. Add the eggs gradually, beating well after each addition. Add a little of the flour if necessary to prevent the mixture from curdling.
3. Sift the remaining flour with the baking powder on to the creamed mixture. Using a large metal spoon, fold in carefully, adding the milk, poppy seeds, vanilla essence and orange zest. Pour into the prepared tin.
4. Bake in the centre of the oven for 1–1$\frac{1}{4}$ hours or until the top springs back when pressed lightly with a fingertip. Cover with a piece of greaseproof paper if the top is getting too dark.
5. Meanwhile, make the glaze by combining the orange juice and sugar in a small saucepan. Bring to the boil, then reduce the heat and simmer for 5 minutes
6. Remove the cake from the oven and allow to cool in the tin for 30 minutes, then turn out on to a wire rack to cool. While still warm, prick holes all over the top with a skewer and pour over the warm glaze. Leave to cool completely.

NOTE: This cake mixture is difficult to cream; it has a high proportion of sugar which makes for an excellent texture.

Upside-down Toffee Gingerbread

This can be served as a cake or a very indulgent winter pudding with Greek yoghurt to accompany.

For the toffee topping
55g/2oz unsalted butter
85g/3oz soft light brown sugar
$1/2$ teaspoon ground ginger
6 dried figs, roughly chopped
8 dried pears
75g/$2^1/_2$oz macadamia nuts

For the gingerbread
melted lard or oil for greasing tin
110g/4oz butter
110g/4oz soft light brown sugar
110g/4oz black treacle
225g/8oz plain flour
2 teaspoons ground ginger
2 eggs, beaten
85ml/3fl oz milk
1 teaspoon bicarbonate of soda
2 tablespoons stem ginger, diced

1. Preheat the oven to 180°C/350°F/gas mark 4. Grease a 20cm/8in moule-à-manqué or round cake tin.
2. Make the toffee topping: melt the butter and stir in the sugar and ginger. Pour into the prepared tin.
3. Arrange the dried fruit and nuts on the toffee.
4. Make the gingerbread: melt the butter, sugar and treacle together in a saucepan over a low heat. Do not let the mixture boil. Remove from the heat and allow to cool.
5. Sift the flour with the ground ginger into a large mixing bowl and make a well in the centre. Pour in the eggs and melted mixture. Using a wooden spoon, gradually draw in the flour and mix to a smooth batter.
6. Warm the milk to blood heat, add the bicarbonate of soda and pour into the batter with the stem ginger. Mix well. Pour carefully on to the fruit and nuts in the prepared tin.
7. Bake in the centre of the oven for about 45 minutes or until a sharp knife or skewer inserted into the centre of the cake comes out clean.
8. While the cake is still warm, turn it upside-down on to a wire rack and leave to cool completely.

Danish Pastries

When rolling out Danish pastry, take care to prevent the butter from breaking through the paste as this makes the resulting pastry heavy. Roll with short, quick, firm rolls and without 'pushing'. Avoid using too much flour. If the paste is becoming warm and unmanageable, wrap it in clingfilm and chill well before proceeding.

15g/½oz fresh yeast
1 tablespoon caster sugar
100ml/3½fl oz lukewarm milk
225g/8oz plain flour
a pinch of salt
1 egg, lightly beaten
110g/4oz unsalted butter, slightly softened

For the almond filling
45g/1½oz butter
45g/1½oz icing sugar
30g/1oz ground almonds
2 drops vanilla essence

For the cinnamon filling
30g/1oz butter
30g/1oz sugar
1 teaspoon ground cinnamon
a handful of mixed dried fruit and chopped mixed peel

For the glaze
1 egg, beaten
110g/4oz icing sugar quantity glacé icing (see page 220)

1. Cream the yeast with 1 teaspoon of the sugar and the milk. Preheat the oven to 200°C/400°F/gas mark 6.
2. Sift the flour with the salt into a mixing bowl. Add the remaining sugar. Make a well in the centre and add the egg and yeast mixture.
3. Mix to a soft dough, using a round-bladed knife to draw in the surrounding flour gradually. If extra liquid is required, add a little more water.
4. When the dough leaves the sides of the bowl, turn it on to a floured work surface and bring together quickly. Roll to a 30 × 15cm/12 × 6in rectangle.
5. Divide the butter into hazelnut-sized pieces and dot over the top two-thirds of the dough, leaving a 1cm/½in clear margin round the edge. Fold the pastry into 3, bringing the bottom unbuttered third up over the centre section first, and then the buttered top third down over it. You now have a thick parcel of pastry. Give it a 90° turn so that the former top edge is on your right. Press the edges lightly together.
6. Dust lightly with flour and roll into a long rectangle again. Fold into 3 as before. Chill for 15 minutes.
7. Roll and fold the pastry once or twice again, turning it in the same direction as before, until the butter is worked in well and the paste does not look streaky. Chill for at least 30 minutes or overnight before proceeding with one of the recipes below.
8. Make the almond filling: cream the butter, add the sugar and beat well until light and soft. Mix in the ground almonds and flavour with vanilla essence. Mix well but do not overbeat or the oil will run from the almonds, making the paste greasy.
9. Make the cinnamon filling: cream the butter, add the sugar and beat well until light and soft. Add the cinnamon, fruit and peel and mix well.
10. Brush with egg glaze and bake in the centre of the oven for 15–20 miniutes.

Leek and Olive Beer Bread Tart

Serves 4
4 large leeks, sliced
55g/2oz butter
1 clove of garlic, crushed
150ml/¼ pint double cream
1 egg yolk
1 whole egg

110g/4oz green olives, pitted and halved
55g/2oz Kalamata olives, pitted and halved
1 teaspoon chopped fresh sage
salt and freshly ground black pepper
225g/8oz quantity beer bread dough (see
    following recipe)
55g/2oz feta cheese, crumbled

1. Preheat the oven to 200°C/400°F/gas mark 6.
2. Wash the leeks thoroughly and dry on kitchen paper. Heat the butter in a large saucepan, add the leeks and cook over a very low heat for about 20 minutes, or until soft but not brown. Add the garlic and continue to cook for a further 5 minutes.
3. Add the cream, bring to the boil and simmer for 5 minutes. Remove from the heat and allow to cool. Add the egg yolk and whole egg, olives and sage and season to taste with salt and pepper. Set aside.
4. Meanwhile, knock back the risen beer bread dough and roll out into a circle about 27.5cm/11in in diameter. Place on a lightly floured baking sheet.
5. Spread the leek mixture over the surface, leaving a 2.5cm/1in border all the way around the edge. Sprinkle over the feta cheese.
6. Bake the tart in the centre of the preheated oven for 30–40 minutes, or until golden-brown and the leek mixture has set. Reduce the oven temperature if the tart shows signs of burning. Serve warm.

BEER BREAD

Makes 1 450g/1lb loaf

55g/2oz butter
2 teaspoons soft light brown sugar
290ml/½ pint brown ale
30g/1oz fresh yeast

2 teaspoons salt
1 egg
225g/8oz wholemeal flour
225g/8oz strong plain white flour

1. Grease a 1kg/2¼lb loaf tin.
2. Bring sugar, beer and remaining butter to boiling point. Cool to lukewarm, then use 1–2 spoonfuls of this liquid to cream the yeast, then add yeast, salt, and lightly beaten egg to the beer mixture.
3. Sift the flours into a warmed large mixing bowl. Make a well in the centre and pour in the liquid. Mix, first with a knife, and then with your fingers, to a soft but not sloppy dough. Knead until very elastic (approx. 10 mins).
4. Return dough to bowl. Cover with oiled clingfilm. Leave in a warm place until it has doubled in bulk, then knead again until smooth. Shape into a loaf shape and put into the tin. Cover again with oiled clingfilm and return to the warm place until doubled in size and the shape of the finished loaf.
5. Meanwhile, preheat the oven to 200°C/400°F/gas mark 6. Bake loaf in middle of oven for 35 minutes, or until it is brown on top and sounds hollow when tapped on the underside. Cool on a wire rack.

RIOJA

MISCELLANEOUS

Red Pepper Salad

Serves 4
4 red peppers
1 clove of garlic
1/2 teaspoon salt
3 tablespoons extra virgin olive oil
4 anchovy fillets
1 teaspoon chopped fresh oregano
3 tablespoons pitted black olives

1. Preheat the grill to its highest setting. Cut the peppers into quarters and remove the membrane and seeds. Grill the skin side of the peppers until they are blistered and blackened all over. Place under running cold water and remove the skins. Cut the flesh into strips.
2. Crush the garlic with the salt and add the oil and anchovies. Mash well together. Add the oregano and toss in the red pepper strips. Mix with the olives.

Sweet Vinegar Rice

This is the recipe for the rice used in sushi. As with any cooked rice dish, keep refrigerated and eat within 24 hours of cooking.

Makes enough for 32 pieces of sushi
225g/8oz Japanese sushi short-grain rice
450ml/3/4 pint water
1 piece of kombu seaweed (see note)
75ml/2 1/2fl oz rice wine vinegar
1 tablespoon caster sugar
2 teaspoons salt

1. Put the rice into a sieve and rinse under running cold water for 1 minute, to remove excess starch.
2. Put into a saucepan, cover with the water, add the kombu and allow to soak for 45 minutes.
3. After the soaking time, cover the saucepan with a well-fitting lid and bring to the boil. Reduce the heat and continue to cook the rice for 10–12 minutes or until cooked through.
4. Meanwhile, put the vinegar into a small saucepan, add the sugar and salt and heat slowly until dissolved. Remove from the heat and allow to cool.
5. When the rice is cooked, turn it on to a flat plate and remove and discard the kombu.
6. Pour the sweetened vinegar over the rice, toss with a fork and allow to cool. Use as required.

Egg Pasta

450g/1lb strong '00' flour
4 large eggs
1 tablespoon oil

1. Sift the flour on to a wooden board. Make a well in the centre and put in the eggs and oil.
2. Using the fingers of one hand, mix together the eggs and oil and gradually draw in the flour, to make a very stiff dough.
3. Knead until smooth and elastic (about 15 minutes). Wrap in clingfilm and leave to relax in a cool place for 1 hour.
4. Roll out one small piece of dough at a time until paper-thin. Cut into the required shape.
5. Allow to dry (unless making ravioli), hanging over a chair back if long noodles, or lying on a wire rack or dry tea towel if small ones, for at least 30 minutes before cooking. Ravioli is dried after stuffing.

NOTE: If more or less pasta is required the recipe can be altered on a pro-rata basis, for example a 340g/12oz quantity of flour calls for a pinch of salt, 3 eggs and 1 scant tablespoon of oil.

Aspic

1 litre/1 1/2 pints very well-flavoured, seasoned white
    stock (see below)
2 egg shells, crushed
2 egg whites
15–30g/1/2–1oz gelatine, as necessary

1. Lift or skim any fat from the stock.
2. Put the stock into a large saucepan and sprinkle on the gelatine. If the stock is liquid when chilled, use 30g/1oz gelatine; if the stock is set when chilled only 15g/1/2oz will be necessary. Put over a gentle heat to dissolve. Allow to cool.
3. Put the shells and egg whites into the stock. Place over the heat and whisk steadily with a balloon whisk until the mixture begins to boil. Stop whisking immediately and draw the pan off the heat. Allow the mixture to subside. Take care not to break the crust formed by the egg white.
4. Bring the aspic just to the boil again, and again allow to subside. Repeat this once more (the egg white will trap the sediment in the stock and clear the aspic). Allow to cool for 2 minutes.
5. Fix a double layer of fine muslin over a clean basin and carefully strain the aspic through it, taking care to hold the egg-white crust back. When all, or almost all, the liquid is through allow the egg white to slip into the muslin. Strain the aspic again – this time through both egg-white crust and cloth. Do not try to hurry the process by squeezing the cloth, or murky aspic will result.

NOTE: When clearing, it is a good idea to scald the saucepan, sieve and whisk before use.

Brown Stock

900g/2lb beef and veal bones
1 onion, peeled and chopped, skin reserved
1 carrot, roughly chopped
1 stick of celery, chopped
green part of 2 leeks, chopped (if available)
parsley stalks

a few mushroom peelings (if available)
2 bay leaves
6 black peppercorns

1. Preheat the oven to 220°C/425°F/gas mark 7.
2. Put the beef bones into a roasting pan and brown in the oven (up to 1 hour).
3. Brown the onion, carrot, celery and leeks, if using, in the oil in a large stock-pot. It is essential that they do not burn.
4. When the bones are well browned, add them to the vegetables with the onion skins, parsley stalks, mushroom peelings, if using, bay leaves and peppercorns. Cover with cold water and bring very slowly to the boil, skimming off any scum as it rises to the surface.
5. When clear of scum, simmer gently for 6–8 hours, or even longer, skimming off the fat as necessary and topping up with water if the level gets very low. The longer it simmers, and the more liquid reduces by evaporation, the stronger the stock will be.
6. Strain, cool and lift off any remaining fat.

NOTE: Lamb stock can be made in the same way with lamb bones but is only suitable for lamb dishes.

White Stock

onion, sliced
celery, sliced
carrot, sliced
chicken or veal bones
parsley
thyme
bay leaf
black peppercorns

1. Put all the ingredients into a saucepan. Cover generously with water and bring to the boil slowly. Skim off any fat, and/or scum.
2. Simmer for 3–4 hours, skimming frequently and topping up the water level if necessary. The liquid should reduce to half the original quantity.
3. Strain, cool and lift off all the fat.

Ham Stock

The best-flavoured ham stock is generally the well-skimmed liquor from boiling a ham or gammon (see note), but this recipe works well with a cooked ham bone.

1 cooked ham bone
1 onion, chopped
1 carrot, chopped
1 bay leaf
fresh parsley stalks
black peppercorns

1. Place all the ingredients together in a large saucepan. Cover with cold water and bring gradually to the boil. Skim off any fat and/or scum.

Simmer for 2–3 hours, skimming frequently and topping up the water level if necessary.
2. Strain and use as required.

NOTE: Ham stock is usually salty and should not be reduced.

Fish Stock

1 onion, sliced
1 carrot, sliced
1 stick of celery, sliced
fish bones, skins and fins, preferably from white flat fish, such as turbot, sole, etc., well rinsed
parsley stalks
1 bay leaf
1 sprig of thyme
black peppercorns

1. Put all the ingredients into a large saucepan.
2. Cover with cold water and bring to the boil, then reduce the heat to a gentle simmer. Cook over a very slow heat for 20–30 minutes.
3. Skim the stock with a large spoon at regular intervals. This prevents fat and impurities boiling into the liquid which can impair the flavour and quality.
4. Strain the stock and use as required.

NOTE: If the stock is allowed to boil it may become cloudy. Do not cook the stock for more than 30 minutes or it may taste bitter.

Bread Sauce

This is a very rich sauce. The quantity of butter may be reduced, and the cream is optional.

1 large onion, peeled
6 cloves
290ml/½ pint milk
1 bay leaf
10 white peppercorns, or a pinch of freshly ground white pepper
a pinch of freshly grated nutmeg
salt
55g/2oz fresh white breadcrumbs
55g/2oz butter
2 tablespoons single cream (optional)

1. Cut the onion in half. Stick the cloves into the onion pieces and put with the milk and bay leaf into a saucepan.
2. Add the peppercorns, nutmeg, and a good pinch of salt. Bring to the boil very slowly, then remove from the heat and leave to infuse for 30 minutes. Strain.
3. Reheat the milk and add the breadcrumbs, butter and the cream, if using. Mix and return to the saucepan.
4. Reheat the sauce carefully without reboiling. If it has become too thick, beat in more hot milk. It should be creamy. Check the seasoning.

Clarified Butter

Method 1: Put the butter into a saucepan with a cupful of water and heat until melted and frothy. Allow to cool and set solid, then lift the butter, now clarified, off the top of the liquid.

Method 2: Heat the butter until foaming without allowing it to burn. Pour it through fine muslin or a double layer of clean 'J' cloth.

Method 3: Melt the butter in a heavy saucepan and skim off the froth with a slotted spoon.

NOTE: Clarified butter will act as a seal on pâtés or potted meats, and is useful for frying as it will withstand great heat before burning.

Mayonnaise

2 egg yolks
salt and freshly ground white pepper
1 teaspoon dry English mustard
290ml/$^1/_2$ pint olive oil, or 150ml/$^1/_4$ pint each olive and salad oil
a squeeze of lemon juice
1 tablespoon white wine vinegar

1. Put the yolks into a bowl with a pinch of salt and the mustard and beat well with a wooden spoon.
2. Add the oil, literally drop by drop, beating all the time. The mixture should be very thick by the time half the oil is added.
3. Beat in the lemon juice.
4. Resume pouring in the oil, going more quickly now, but alternating the dribbles of oil with small quantities of vinegar.
5. Season to taste with salt and pepper.

NOTE: If the mixture curdles, another egg yolk should be beaten in a separate bowl, and the curdled mixture beaten into it drop by drop.

French Dressing (Vinaigrette)

45ml/3 tablespoons salad oil
15ml/1 tablespoon wine vinegar
salt and pepper

Put all the ingredients into a screw-top jar. Before using, shake until well emulsified.

NOTES: This dressing can be flavoured with crushed garlic, mustard, a pinch of sugar, chopped fresh herbs, etc., as desired.
   If kept refrigerated, the dressing will more easily form an emulsion when whisked or shaken, and has a slightly thicker consistency.

Salsa Pizzaiola

1 onion, chopped
2 tablespoons olive oil
3–4 cloves of garlic, chopped
1kg/2$^1/_4$lb canned plum tomatoes
2 tablespoons tomato purée
2 teaspoons dried oregano
1 teaspoon dried basil
1 bay leaf
2 teaspoons sugar
salt and freshly ground black pepper

1. In a saucepan, sweat the onion in the oil until transparent.
2. Add the garlic and cook for 1 further minute, then stir in the tomatoes with their liquid, the tomato purée, oregano, basil, bay leaf, and sugar. Season to taste with salt and pepper. Bring to the boil, then cook very gently for about 1 hour.
3. Remove the bay leaf and check the seasoning. This sauce should be quite thick and rough but you may purée it if you wish.

Salsa Verde

$^1/_2$ cucumber, deseeded and diced
$^1/_2$ green chilli, finely diced
1 shallot, finely chopped
grated zest and juice of 1 lime
1 teaspoon caster sugar
1 tablespoon chopped coriander
1 tablespoon good-quality olive oil
salt and freshly ground black pepper

1. Mix together all the ingredients and season to taste with salt and pepper. Chill for 2 hours before serving.

Pesto Sauce

2 cloves of garlic
2 large cups of fresh basil leaves
55g/2oz pinenuts
55g/2oz Parmesan cheese, freshly grated
150ml/$^1/_4$ pint olive oil
salt

1. In a blender or mortar, grind the garlic and basil together to a paste. Add the nuts, cheese, oil and plenty of salt. Keep in a covered jar in a cool place.

NOTE: Pesto is sometimes made with walnuts instead of pinenuts, and the nuts may be pounded with the other ingredients to give a smooth paste.

Red Pesto

55g/2oz dried sun-dried tomatoes
2 cloves of garlic, peeled
1 small bunch basil
3 tablespoons good-quality olive oil
30g/1oz pecorino cheese, finely grated
salt and freshly ground black pepper

1. Rinse the tomatoes, then soak in warm water for 20 minutes, or until soft. When ready, drain, dry and chop. Discard the liquid.
2. In a liquidizer or mortar, grind the garlic and basil together to a paste.
3. Whizz in the tomatoes, then add the oil slowly with the motor still running. Whizz in the cheese quickly.
4. Season with salt and pepper.

Curry Powder

There is no beating freshly made curry powder. Toasting and blending all the spices together makes a very good blend that can be used for all our recipes specifying curry powder. This mixture is quite hot: to increase or lessen the heat, adjust the quantity of chillies accordingly. The art of good curry powders is in the toasting; when the seeds are split by the heat, their full flavour comes through. Take care not to burn the seeds or the powder will taste bitter.

To keep the curry powder fresh it is best stored in the freezer or a cool, dark place. Use within 3 months; any longer and the spices lose their flavour.

This quantity makes enough powder for several curries, halve the amount of seeds to make a smaller quantity. The spices can be bought from specialist grocers and some supermarkets.

6 tablespoons coriander seeds
4 tablespoons cumin seeds
6 dried red chillies
1 tablespoon black peppercorns
1 tablespoon mustard seeds, preferably black
3 tablespoons ground turmeric
3 teaspoons ground fenugreek

1. Heat a large frying pan. Add the coriander seeds and toss and toast over a medium heat until they begin to pop and colour. Transfer to a plate to cool.
2. Add the cumin seeds and chillies and toast in the same way until the cumin pops and the chillies turn dark reddish-brown in colour. Add them to the coriander and allow to cool.
3. Toast the peppercorns and mustard seeds individually in the same way and allow to cool.
4. When all the seeds are cold, put into a spice/coffee grinder or mortar. Pound together until a fine powder is formed. Stir the turmeric and fenugreek into the powder. Transfer to an airtight container and store until required.

Choux Pastry

85g/3oz butter
200ml/7fl oz water
105g/3¾oz plain flour, well sifted
a pinch of salt
3 eggs

1. Put the butter and water into a heavy saucepan. Bring slowly to the boil so that by the time the water boils the butter is completely melted.
2. Immediately the mixture is boiling really fast, tip in all the flour with the salt and remove the pan from the heat.
3. Working as fast as you can, beat the mixture hard with the wooden spoon: it will soon become thick and smooth and leave the sides of the pan.
4. Stand the bottom of the saucepan in a bowl or sink of cold water to speed up the cooling process.
5. When the mixture is cool, beat in the eggs, a little at a time, until it is soft, shiny and smooth. If the eggs are large, it may not be necessary to add all of them. The mixture should be of a dropping consistency – not too runny. ('Dropping consistency' means that the mixture will fall off a spoon rather reluctantly, and all in a blob; if it runs off, it is too wet, and if it will not fall even when the spoon is jerked slightly, it is too thick.)
6. Use as required.

Puff Pastry

225g/8oz plain flour
a pinch of salt
30g/1oz lard
120–150ml/4–5fl oz iced water
140–200g/5–7oz butter

1. If you have never made puff pastry before, use the smaller amount of butter: this will give a normal pastry. If you have some experience, more butter will produce a lighter, very rich pastry.
2. Sift the flour with the salt into a large bowl. Rub in the lard. Add enough water to mix with a knife to a doughy consistency. Turn on to a floured board and knead quickly until just smooth. Chill, wrapped, in the refrigerator for 30 minutes.
3. Lightly flour the board and roll the dough into a rectangle about 30 × 10cm/12 × 4in.
4. Tap the butter lightly with a floured rolling pin to shape it into a flattened block about 9 × 8cm/3½ × 3in. Put the butter on the rectangle of pastry and fold both ends over to enclose it. Fold the third closest to you over first and then bring the top third down. Press the sides together to prevent the butter escaping. Give it a 90-degree anti-clockwise turn so that the folded, closed edge is on your left.
5. Now tap the pastry parcel with the rolling pin to flatten the butter a little; then roll out, quickly and lightly, until the pastry is 3 times as long as it is wide. Fold it very evenly in 3, first folding the third closest to you over, then bringing the top third down. Give it a 90-degree anti-clockwise turn so that the folded, closed edge is on your left. Again press the edges firmly with the rolling pin. Then roll out again to form a rectangle as before.
6. Now the pastry has had 2 rolls and folds, or

217

'turns' as they are called. It should be put to rest in a cool place for 30 minutes or so. The rolling and folding must be repeated twice more, the pastry again rested, and then again given 2 more turns. This makes a total of 6 turns. If the butter is still very streaky, roll and fold it once more.

Rich Shortcrust Pastry

170g/6oz plain flour
pinch of salt
85g/3oz butter
1 egg yolk
very cold water

1. Sift the flour with the salt.
2. Rub in the butter until the mixture looks like breadcrumbs.
3. Mix the yolk with 30ml/2 tablespoons water and add to the mixture.
4. Mix to a firm dough, first with a knife, and finally with one hand. It may be necessary to add more water, but the pastry should not be too damp. (Though crumbly pastry is more difficult to handle, it produces a shorter, lighter result.)
5. Chill, wrapped, for 30 minutes before using, or allow to relax after rolling out but before baking.

NOTE: To make sweet rich shortcrust pastry, mix in 15ml/1 tablespoon caster sugar once the fat has been rubbed into the flour.

Martha Stewart's Walnut Pastry

225g/8oz plain flour
a pinch of salt
100g/4oz butter
140g/5oz ground walnuts
45g/1½oz sugar
1 egg, beaten

1. Sift the flour with the salt into a large bowl. Rub in the butter until the mixture resembles coarse breadcrumbs. Add the walnuts.
2. Stir in the sugar and add enough beaten egg (probably half an egg) to just bind the mixture together. Knead lightly. Chill, wrapped, in the refrigerator before use.

NOTES: If you have a food processor, simply beat all the ingredients together until lightly combined. Chill before use.
    This pastry is virtually impossible to roll out: simply press into place.

Brandy Snap Cups

Makes 8
110g/4oz caster sugar
110g/4oz butter
4 tablespoons golden syrup
110g/4oz plain flour

juice of ½ lemon
a large pinch of ground ginger

To serve
whipped cream or ice cream

1. Preheat the oven to 190°C/375°F/gas mark 5. Grease a baking sheet, a palette knife and one end of a wide rolling pin or a narrow jam jar or bottle.
2. Melt the sugar, butter and syrup together in a saucepan. Remove from the heat.
3. Sift in the flour, stirring well. Add the lemon juice and ginger.
4. Place teaspoonfuls of the mixture on the prepared baking sheet about 15cm/6in apart. Bake in the preheated oven for 5–7 minutes until golden-brown and still soft. Watch carefully as they burn easily. Remove from the oven.
5. When cool enough to handle, lever each biscuit off the baking sheet with a greased palette knife.
6. Working quickly, shape around the end of the rolling pin or greased jam jar to form a cup-shaped mould.
7. When the biscuits have been shaped, remove them and leave to cool on a wire rack.
8. Serve filled with whipped cream or ice cream.

NOTES: If the brandy snaps are not to be served immediately, once cool they must be put into an airtight container for storage or they will become soggy. Similarly, brandy snaps should not be filled with moist mixtures like whipped cream or ice cream until shortly before serving, or they will quickly lose their crispness.
    Do not bake too many snaps at one time as once they become cold they are too brittle to shape. They can be made pliable again if returned to the oven.

Mincemeat

This mincemeat does not keep well – if you want to preserve it, omit the banana and add it just before using the mincemeat.

Makes just over 450g/1lb
1 small cooking apple, washed and cored
55g/2oz butter
85g/3oz sultanas
85g/3oz raisins
85g/3oz currants
45g/1½oz mixed peel, chopped
45g/1½oz chopped almonds
grated rind of large lemon
2.5ml/½ teaspoon mixed spice
15ml/1 tablespoon brandy
85g/3oz brown sugar
1 banana, chopped

Grate the apple, skin and all. Melt the butter and add it, with all the other ingredients, to the apple. Mix well.

Pâte Sablée

285g/10oz plain flour
a pinch of salt
225g/8oz butter, softened
2 egg yolks
110g/4oz icing sugar, sifted
2 drops of vanilla essence

1. Sift the flour with the salt on to a board. Make a large well in the centre and put the butter in it. Place the egg yolks and sugar on the butter with the vanilla essence.
2. Using the fingertips of one hand, 'peck' the butter, yolks and sugar together. When mixed to a soft paste, draw in the flour and knead lightly until the pastry is just smooth.
3. Wrap and chill before rolling or pressing out to the required shape. Then chill again.

Crème Pâtissière

290ml/½ pint milk
2 egg yolks
55g/2oz caster sugar
20g/¾oz plain flour
20g/¾oz cornflour
vanilla essence

1. Scald the milk by bringing it to just below boiling point in a saucepan.
2. Cream the egg yolks with the sugar and a little of the milk and when pale, mix in the flours. Pour on the milk and mix well.
3. Return the mixture to the pan and bring slowly to the boil, stirring continuously. (It will go alarmingly lumpy, but don't worry, keep stirring vigorously and it will become smooth.) Allow to cool slightly, then add the vanilla essence.

Crème Anglaise (English Egg Custard)

290ml/½ pint milk
1 vanilla pod or a few drops of vanilla essence
2 egg yolks
1 tablespoon caster sugar

1. Heat the milk and vanilla pod, if using, and bring slowly to the boil.
2. Beat the yolks in a bowl with the sugar. Remove the vanilla pod, and pour the milk on to the egg yolks, stirring steadily. Mix well and return to the pan.
3. Stir over a low heat until the mixture thickens sufficiently to coat the back of a spoon (about 5 minutes). Do not boil. Strain into a chilled bowl.
4. Add the vanilla essence, if using.

Orange Marmalade Crème Anglaise

150ml/¼ pint milk
150ml/¼ pint whipping cream
2 egg yolks
3 tablespoons Seville orange marmalade, chopped
1 tablespoon Cointreau

1. Heat the milk with the cream in a heavy based saucepan and bring slowly to the boil.
2. Beat the egg yolks and marmalade together until pale.
3. Pour the milk and cream mixture on to the egg yolks, stirring steadily.
4. Return the mixture to the pan and cook over a low heat, stirring well with a wooden spoon, for about 5 minutes, or until the custard is thick enough to coat the back of the spoon. Do not allow to boil.
5. Pour into a chilled bowl and add the Cointreau. Allow to cool before using.

Cinnamon Crème Anglaise

Serves 4
290ml/½ pint milk
290ml/½ pint whipping cream
2 cinnamon sticks
3 egg yolks
4 tablespoons caster sugar

1. Put the milk, cream and cinnamon sticks into a heavy-based saucepan and bring to scalding point. Remove from the heat and allow to infuse for 30 minutes.
2. Beat the egg yolks and sugar together in a bowl until light and frothy. Strain the infused milk mixture on top and stir together.
3. Return to the rinsed-out pan and bring back to scalding point over a low heat, stirring constantly with a wooden spoon, until the custard is slightly thickened and will just coat the back of the spoon. Do not allow the mixture to boil or it will curdle. Strain into a clean bowl and serve hot, warm or chilled.

Kumquat and Date Compote

Serves 4
225g/8oz kumquats
225g/8oz dates
170g/6oz caster sugar
150ml/¼ pint water
1 cinnamon stick
3 tablespoons Armagnac

1. Wash the kumquats and slice them thinly, removing any pips. Cut the dates in half and remove the stones.
2. Dissolve the sugar in the water, bring to the boil and add the cinnamon stick. Lower the heat and simmer for 5–7 minutes, or until syrupy.

3. Add the kumquats and simmer for 2 minutes. Add the dates and cook for a further 2 minutes.
4. Remove the cinnamon and add the Armagnac. Serve warm or chilled.

Raspberry Coulis

340g/12oz raspberries
juice of $\frac{1}{2}$ lemon
70ml/2$\frac{1}{2}$fl oz sugar syrup (see below)

1. Whizz all the ingredients together in a food processor or blender, and push through a conical strainer.

NOTE: If it is too thin, the coulis can be thickened by boiling rapidly in a heavy saucepan. Stir well to prevent it catching.

Apricot Glaze

3 tablespoons apricot jam
2 tablespoons water
juice of $\frac{1}{2}$ lemon

1. Place all the ingredients in a heavy saucepan.
2. Bring slowly to the boil, stirring gently (avoid beating in bubbles) until syrupy in consistency. Strain.

NOTE: Use when still warm, as the glaze becomes too stiff to manage when cold. It will keep warm standing over a saucepan of very hot water.

Glacé Icing

225g/8oz icing sugar
boiling water to mix

1. Sift the icing sugar into a bowl.
2. Add enough boiling water to mix to a fairly stiff coating consistency. The icing should hold a trail when dropped from a spoon but gradually find its own level. It needs surprisingly little water.

NOTE: Hot water produces a shinier icing than cold. Also, the icing, on drying, is less likely to craze, crack or become watery if made with boiling water.

Sugar Syrup

285g/10oz granulated sugar
570ml/1 pint water
thinly pared zest of 1 lemon

1. Put the sugar, water and lemon zest into a saucepan and heat slowly until the sugar has completely dissolved.
2. Bring to the boil and cook to the required consistency (see below). Allow to cool.
3. Strain. Keep covered in a cool place until needed.

NOTE: Sugar syrup will keep unrefrigerated for about 5 days, and for several weeks if kept chilled.

STAGES IN SUGAR SYRUP CONCENTRATION

TYPE OF SUGAR SYRUP	BOILING POINT	USES
Vaseline	107°C/220°–221°F	Syrup and sorbets
Short thread	108°C/225°–226°F	Syrup and mousse-based ice creams
Long thread	110°C/230°–235°F	Syrup
Soft ball	115°C/235°–240°F	Fondant, fudge
Firm ball	120°C/248°–250°F	Italian meringue
Hard ball	124°C/255°–265°F	Marshmallows
Soft crack	138°C/270°–290°F	Soft toffee
Hard crack	155°C/300°–310°F	Hard toffee and some nougat
	160°C/318°F	Nougat
Spun sugar	152°C/305°–308°F	Spun sugar

INDEX